U.S. ARMS SALES

Studies in Defense Policy
TITLES IN PRINT

STUDIES IN DEFENSE POLICY

U.S. ARMS SALES

The China-Taiwan Tangle

A. Doak Barnett

THE BROOKINGS INSTITUTION
Washington, D.C.

THE BROOKINGS INSTITUTION is an independent organization devoted to nonpartisan research, education, and publication in economics, government, foreign policy, and the social sciences generally. Its principal purposes are to aid in the development of sound public policies and to promote public understanding of issues of national importance.

The Institution was founded on December 8, 1927, to merge the activities of the Institute for Government Research, founded in 1916, the Institute of Economics, founded in 1922, and the Robert Brookings Graduate School of Economics and Government, founded in 1924.

The Board of Trustees is responsible for the general administration of the Institution, while the immediate direction of the policies, program, and staff is vested in the President, assisted by an advisory committee of the officers and staff. The by-laws of the Institution state: "It is the function of the Trustees to make possible the conduct of scientific research, and publication, under the most favorable conditions, and to safeguard the independence of the research staff in the pursuit of their studies and in the publication of the results of such studies. It is not a part of their function to determine, control, or influence the conduct of particular investigations or the conclusions reached."

The President bears final responsibility for the decision to publish a manuscript as a Brookings book. In reaching his judgment on the competence, accuracy, and objectivity of each study, the President is advised by the director of the appropriate research program and weighs the views of a panel of expert outside readers who report to him in confidence on the quality of the work. Publication of a work signifies that it is deemed a competent treatment worthy of public consideration but does not imply endorsement of conclusions or recommendations.

The Institution maintains its position of neutrality on issues of public policy in order to safeguard the intellectual freedom of the staff. Hence interpretations or conclusions in Brookings publications should be understood to be solely those of the authors and should not be attributed to the Institution, to its trustees, officers, or other staff members, or to the organizations that support its research.

FOREWORD

In contemporary international relations, arms sales have increasingly been used for political purposes, as well as military ones. Experience suggests, however, that such sales are no substitute for diplomacy and sound policy. At times they create more problems than they solve. Recent developments in U.S. relations with China and Taiwan corroborate this observation.

Washington and Beijing normalized political relations at the start of 1979, and in the ensuing two years remarkable progress was made in developing economic and other ties between the two countries. In mid-1981 the U.S. government announced that it had decided to authorize the sale of weapons to China on a case-by-case basis. Washington's aim was to build a significant strategic relationship with Beijing.

However, just before this U.S. announcement, the Chinese Ministry of Foreign Affairs announced that it was not interested in buying U.S. arms if Washington continued arms sales to Taiwan. During 1981–82 tensions over U.S. arms sales to Taiwan steadily grew, threatening to create a serious political crisis that could lead to a downgrading of U.S.-China diplomatic relations. As of May 1982 it was still unclear whether a major setback in relations would occur or whether the dispute could be defused by compromise.

In this staff paper, A. Doak Barnett, a senior fellow in the Brookings Foreign Policy Studies program, analyzes how this situation evolved, assesses the basic elements in the dispute, and discusses Washington's policy options. He argues that attempting to develop significant military ties with China before U.S.-China political relations are on a sound, sustainable basis is "putting the cart before the horse," and that U.S.-China political relations will remain uncertain and fragile until there is further compromise and progress on the Taiwan issue. He maintains that the situation calls for great restraint in U.S. military relations (including arms sales) with both China and Taiwan.

This paper, the twenty-seventh in the Brookings series of Studies in Defense Policy, was edited by Nancy D. Davidson, verified by Clifford A. Wright, and typed by Robert L. Londis. Brookings gratefully acknowledges financial support from the Henry Luce Foundation and the Ford Foundation. The views expressed here are the author's alone, and should not be ascribed to either the Henry Luce Foundation or the Ford Foundation or to the trustees, officers, or other staff members of the Brookings Institution.

BRUCE K. MAC LAURY
President

May 1982
Washington, D.C.

U.S. ARMS SALES

The China-Taiwan Tangle

A. Doak Barnett

The normalization of U.S.-China relations in the 1970s contributed significantly to both American and Chinese security interests. On balance, it
clearly improved the prospects for stability in most of East Asia.

The impact of this major shift in international alignments was not entirely positive, however. Improvement in Washington-Beijing relations was
accompanied by—and in many respects it intensified—growing Soviet concerns about trends that leaders in Moscow viewed as threatening. The
already complex triangular relationship among the United States, China,
and the Soviet Union became even more complicated. Moscow increased
its military power and political activities in East Asia, Sino-Soviet and
U.S.-Soviet competition was stepped up in many areas, and conflict involving these and other powers was intensified in the Indochina region.

Nevertheless, U.S.-China détente altered the political scene in East Asia
—and, to a lesser extent, globally—in many favorable ways. It encouraged
the development of more normal relationships between China and most of
its neighbors and lessened tensions in numerous areas (with the notable
exception of the Indochina region) that for years had been actual or potential crisis zones.

During the 1970s, China turned outward to a degree unprecedented
since the Communist takeover in 1949. While continuing to identify itself
with the third world, as it had for many years,[1] China now rapidly expanded friendly ties with all of the major non-Communist industrial nations—Japan and the Western European nations as well as the United
States. It energetically cultivated good relations with the non-Communist
nations to its south that belonged to the Association of South East Asian

1. Starting in 1974, Chinese officials called their country a socialist developing third world
nation. "Chairman of Chinese Delegation Teng Hsiao-Ping's Speech," *Peking Review*, no. 16
(April 19, 1974), p. 11.

1

Nations (ASEAN). It abandoned past rhetoric about "liberation" of Taiwan and adopted a new policy of attraction much more flexible and conciliatory than any pursued in the past. In Korea, while continuing to give full political support to the reunification proposals advocated by the North, it stressed the necessity for reunification to be accomplished peacefully.

More broadly, after acquiring the China seat in the United Nations, and especially after adopting a new modernization program within China following Mao's death in 1976, China's leadership, led by Deng Xiaoping, proclaimed an "open door" policy calling for greatly increased foreign trade as well as much broader cultural, educational, scientific, and technical ties with other nations.[2] It also decided to join organizations such as the International Monetary Fund and World Bank and generally to play an increasingly active role in the international community. Deng and his closest supporters decided, in effect, to "join the world" to an extent no previous Chinese Communist leaders had considered feasible and desirable.

U.S.-China ties multiplied during the 1970s at a pace that few observers would have thought possible at the start of the decade. Especially after full normalization of diplomatic relations on January 1, 1979, high-level political consultations became commonplace; trade soared; scientific, technical, and cultural exchanges rapidly broadened; and contacts of many kinds, at almost all levels of the two governments and societies, began to create the beginnings of new webs of interlocking interests between the two countries.

The Security Motives for U.S.-China Détente

From the time that the first steps were taken to establish contacts between the two countries, the top leaders in both Beijing and Washington were strongly motivated by broad geopolitical and security concerns. Chairman Mao Zedong and Premier Zhou Enlai, the prime movers of Chinese policy, decided, probably in late 1968 or early 1969 (following Soviet intervention in Czechoslovakia), that the Soviet Union had become the major potential threat to China's security.[3] They concluded that an opening to the United States would alter the international "correlation of forces" to China's advantage and create a new counterweight to Soviet

2. "Why China Has Opened Its Doors," *Bangkok Post*, February 10, 1980, in U.S. Foreign Broadcast Information Service, *Daily Report: People's Republic of China*, February 12, 1980, pp. L1–L5 (hereafter cited as FBIS, *Daily Report: PRC*).

3. See A. Doak Barnett, *China and the Major Powers in East Asia* (Brookings Institution, 1977), pp. 49 and 349, note 88.

power. President Richard M. Nixon and national security adviser Henry Kissinger believed that an opening to China could have major favorable effects on the world balance of power. (Nixon extravagantly referred to his visit to China in 1972 as the week that changed the world.) Their aim was to create a new pattern of triangular diplomacy that would give Washington increased leverage in dealing with Moscow—and Beijing too.[4] In addition, they hoped that steps to end two decades of hostile Sino-American confrontation would limit the damage to U.S. interests that might result from an American withdrawal from Vietnam and a general reduction of U.S. forces in East Asia.

During the first years of renewed U.S.-China ties, leaders in both Washington and Beijing viewed the security benefits flowing from the new Sino-American relationship primarily in political and diplomatic terms. There was no sign at that time that either side considered concrete military ties to be feasible. It was only in 1978, on the eve of full normalization of diplomatic relations, that the leadership in the two countries—President Jimmy Carter and Vice Premier Deng Xiaoping—tentatively began to consider contacts in the military field. Washington started a process that was to lead ultimately to U.S. offers to sell first military-related technology and then arms to the Chinese.

Following the U.S.-China opening of 1971–72, it was evident that Beijing hoped to encourage formation of a worldwide anti-Soviet united front. Mao himself took the lead in first urging such a coalition, which he hoped would include all the major non-Communist industrial powers, as well as China and third world nations, to oppose Moscow. However, it is unlikely that Mao or any other top Chinese leaders ever envisaged the development of intimate military cooperation between China and these nations. Beijing's concept of a united front called essentially for a loose political alignment of all nations outside the Soviet Union's sphere of influence to encourage parallel actions aimed at checking Soviet expansionism.

Almost certainly, the Chinese leadership never seriously considered the possibility of forming any specific military alliances with non-Communist powers—or probably even any close operational coordination of military-security policies with them—in the context of such a united front. Having been badly burned, from their perspective, in their earlier alliance relations with Moscow, Chinese leaders had acquired a strong belief in the need to be self-reliant and to avoid weakening their capacity for independent decision-

4. Henry Kissinger, *White House Years* (Little, Brown, 1979), pp. 691, 716–17, 735, 763–70.

making and action, especially in the military-security field. (However, by the late 1970s they were increasingly prepared to develop certain foreign economic ties that gradually involved them in new relationships of international economic interdependence.) In a united front directed against Moscow, China would make its contribution essentially by acting independently, tying down Soviet forces in Asia, and pursuing long-established policies aimed at countering Soviet influence.

Beijing obviously hoped, however, that in promoting a united front policy it could encourage other powers—especially the United States—to increase their military strength in ways that would counterbalance and check Soviet power. It urged the United States and others to be more active in their efforts to oppose Moscow's ambitions—just as earlier in the 1950s (when Beijing viewed the Americans as the main threat to China's security) it had tried to induce Moscow to adopt a harder line and to take greater risks in order to counterbalance and check the United States.

Despite the fact that they thought primarily in terms of a loose political *alignment*—not an alliance or close military cooperation—when urging the formation of an anti-Soviet united front, Chinese leaders *did* hope to obtain access to Western military technology and weapons. They had begun to investigate seriously possible purchases of military technology and arms from Western European nations in the early 1970s.[5] When China's leaders announced the start of their new modernization program in 1978, they declared that the task of upgrading the country's military establishment was (not surprisingly) to be one of China's "four modernizations." From 1978 on, they stepped up their window shopping for military equipment in the West. Briefly it appeared that Beijing's leaders were considering immediate and large-scale purchases of European weapons. At the same time—even prior to normalization of U.S.-China relations—they began to hint, at first subtly, then openly, that they also desired to obtain access to American military technology and weapons.

It was also in 1978, following the Carter administration's decision to move rapidly to complete the process of normalizing U.S.-China relations, that the United States began to put increasing emphasis on the potential military-security importance of U.S.-China ties and started edging toward establishing initial military contacts. In the opinion of many, this was entirely logical in light of the fact that security concerns—at least in the broad geopolitical sense—had been the most important single factor motivating American leaders to explore the possibility of détente with China.

5. Harry G. Gelber, *Technology, Defense, and External Relations in China, 1975–1978* (Boulder, Colo.: Westview Press, 1979), pp. 49–88, 141–81.

Even before the Kissinger and Nixon trips to China, U.S. leaders had attempted to use their political influence to deter any possible Soviet attack on China, which they believed would have very destabilizing effects internationally. In 1969, when major clashes occurred on the Sino-Soviet border and many analysts in Washington felt that there was a real danger that Moscow might take major military action against the Chinese, American leaders warned publicly of the broader dangers that a Sino-Soviet conflict could create.[6] Soon thereafter, in 1970, the Americans rejected a Soviet feeler about a possible agreement on "joint action" to deter any other nuclear power taking "provocative actions" (meaning China).[7]

Then, in the Shanghai Communiqué, issued at the conclusion of the meeting of President Nixon and Premier Zhou in February 1972, the United States and China jointly pledged to oppose "hegemonism" (meaning the Soviet Union).[8] From then on, agreement on the need to check Soviet expansionism was a fundamental, and constant, element in the developing U.S.-China relationship. (However, American leaders repeatedly asserted that Washington's aim was to develop good relations with both Moscow and Beijing, emphasizing that the United States had no intention of using one against the other.)

As U.S.-China political relations gradually improved from 1972 on (with ups and downs), there was also a gradual increase in the stake in broad security terms, as well as bilateral political and economic interests, that U.S. leaders saw in the relationship. However, during the mid-1970s, when progress toward establishing formal diplomatic ties temporarily stalled, U.S.-China security cooperation consisted mainly of parallel denunciations of Moscow's increasing assertiveness abroad.

Normalization and Steps toward Security Links

In the second year of President Carter's administration a new dynamic in the relationship started to develop, with the United States taking the primary initiative. It led step by step not only to full normalization of

6. See, for example, "Secretary Rogers' News Conference of April 7," *Department of State Bulletin*, vol. 60, no. 1557 (April 28, 1969), p. 361; Under Secretary of State Elliot L. Richardson, "The Foreign Policy of the Nixon Administration: Its Aims and Strategy," *Department of State Bulletin*, vol. 61, no. 1578 (September 22, 1969), p. 260.

7. John Newhouse, *Cold Dawn: The Story of SALT* (Holt, Rinehart, and Winston, 1973), p. 189.

8. "Text of Joint Communiqué, Issued at Shanghai, February 27," *Department of State Bulletin*, vol. 66, no. 1708 (March 20, 1972), pp. 435–38.

diplomatic relations, followed by a rapid expansion of political and economic ties, but also to increasing emphasis on mutual security interests. Ultimately there was a series of U.S. decisions—by the Carter administration in 1980 and by the Reagan administration in 1981—which authorized, first, sales to China of "dual-use technology" of possible military use, then sales of nonlethal military support equipment, and, finally, sales of actual weapons. By mid-1981, Washington appeared to have laid a basis for at least one important element in a possible military relationship with the Chinese, the selective transfer of some modern American military technology and equipment to China.

The most important signal that the United States was initiating a more activist China policy was the trip to China by Carter's national security adviser, Zbigniew Brzezinski, in May 1978. While in Beijing, Brzezinski not only informed China's leaders that Carter wished to move ahead soon to achieve full normalization of diplomatic relations; he also declared that a "secure and strong" China is in the U.S. national interest. Underlining the importance of common American and Chinese strategic views, he denounced countries that send "international marauders" abroad (that is, the Soviet Union).[9]

Brzezinski's trip was followed by a period of intense negotiations that finally led in mid-December to agreement that full diplomatic ties would be established at the start of 1979. Throughout 1978, President Carter and Secretary of State Cyrus R. Vance continued to assert that the United States had no intention of playing China against the Soviet Union, and in July Vance repeated earlier denials that the United States intended to provide weapons to China.[10] However, in November it was announced that Washington would not try to prevent Western European nations from selling defensive arms to China.[11] Gradually, the United States was moving away from an "evenhanded" policy toward both Beijing and Moscow, and there was increasing speculation that expanded U.S.-China ties conceivably might have a military dimension.

Following full normalization of relations, there was an immediate increase in visits of high officials between the two countries. Deng Xiaoping

9. National Security Adviser Zbigniew Brzezinski, excerpts from toasts, Peking, May 20 and 22, 1978, in Department of State, Bureau of Public Affairs, Office of Public Communication, *U.S. Policy Toward China, July 15, 1971–January 15, 1979*, Selected Documents, no. 9 (Government Printing Office, 1979), pp. 38–39.

10. Secretary of State Cyrus R. Vance, excerpt from a news conference, July 10, 1978, in ibid., pp. 41–42.

11. Secretary of State Cyrus R. Vance, excerpts from a news conference, November 3, 1978, in ibid., p. 44.

himself journeyed to Washington in early 1979, shortly before China launched its brief punitive invasion of Vietnam (to "teach Vietnam a lesson" for aligning with the Soviet Union and invading Kampuchea). Even though Washington expressed its disapproval of this military action, many observers felt that Deng had successfully played his "American card" to reduce the danger that Moscow would retaliate against China for its attack on Vietnam.

Symbolically, the most important American visit to Beijing during the year after normalization was that of Vice-President Walter Mondale. Although during his trip Mondale placed special emphasis on the importance of expanding economic ties, declaring that a "strong and secure and modernizing China is . . . in the American interest," at the same time he went somewhat further than Brzezinski in stressing the "mutual security" significance of U.S.-China relations. "Any nation which seeks to weaken or isolate you in world affairs," he told the Chinese, "assumes a stance counter to American interests."[12] Mondale publicly reiterated Washington's longstanding official position that it was not considering any anti-Soviet coalition or alliance, and he declared that "we do not have nor do we anticipate a military relationship."[13] However, during his trip the Americans reportedly did indicate to the Chinese that Washington was now considering the adoption of a more flexible policy on the sale to China of dual-use technology for civilian purposes.

The first low-level contacts between American and Chinese military personnel occurred not long after diplomatic ties were normalized, and the two countries soon agreed to exchange military attachés. In the fall of 1979, when U.S.-Soviet tensions were on the rise as a result of the presence of Soviet troops in Cuba, Washington announced that Secretary of Defense Harold Brown would visit China in January 1980.[14]

Offers of Dual-Use Technology and Arms

In December 1979, just before Brown's trip, the Soviet Union invaded Afghanistan, which caused profound shock in Washington. The U.S. government responded with sanctions against Moscow and various other coun-

12. From speech text, in "Vice President: Visit to East Asia," *Department of State Bulletin*, vol. 79, no. 2031 (October 1979), pp. 10–12.

13. See James P. Sterba, "Mondale Says Talks in Peking Put Ties on a Concrete Basis," *New York Times*, August 29, 1979.

14. George C. Wilson, "Defense Chief to Visit China for First Time," *Washington Post*, October 2, 1979.

teractions. Suddenly, Brown's trip acquired a "new dimension" and Washington decided to take one more step in the direction of developing security links with Beijing.[15]

On arrival in Beijing, Brown announced that the United States was interested in developing "wider cooperation on security matters," and before leaving China he revealed (on the basis of decisions made just before he had left Washington) that the United States would now consider Chinese requests to purchase some types of dual-use technology that could have military applications.[16] Immediately following his return, in late January, the U.S. government moved a step further and announced that it was prepared to sell nonlethal military support equipment to Beijing.[17] In March, the State Department published a fairly long list of items—certain types of aircraft, helicopters, radars, instruments, and equipment—that could be considered for sale to the Chinese on a case-by-case basis.[18]

In May, Brown's trip to China was reciprocated by a visit to Washington by Vice Premier Geng Biao, secretary-general of the Chinese Communist party's Military Affairs Commission (and soon to become Beijing's minister of defense). Geng was told that, under the new U.S. policy on technology sales to China, Washington would consider licensing the building of plants in China to manufacture items such as transport helicopters and computer circuits.[19]

Also in 1980, the United States and China secretly began joint operation of two stations in northwest China to monitor Soviet missile tests, using American technology but Chinese personnel (a fact not reported in the U.S. press until mid-1981).[20] This move—which was of obvious benefit to both countries—was the most concrete step toward practical cooperation in the military field taken up to that time—or since.

15. Richard Burt, "U.S. Looks to China for Aid to Pakistan," *New York Times*, January 3, 1980.

16. Fox Butterfield, "Brown, in Peking, Urges Cooperation to Counter Moscow," *New York Times*, January 7, 1980; and Jay Mathews, "U.S., China to Strengthen Afghan Area, Brown Says," *Washington Post*, January 10, 1980.

17. Bernard Gwertzman, "U.S., In New Rebuff to Soviet, Announces It Will Sell China Military Support Equipment," *New York Times*, January 25, 1980.

18. Department of State, Bureau of Public Affairs, *Munitions Control Newsletter*, no. 81 (March 1980). See also Michael Getler, "U.S. Willing to Sell China Copters, Transport Planes," *Washington Post*, March 19, 1980.

19. "U.S. Clears Way to Sell Military Gear to China," *Washington Post*, May 30, 1980.

20. See "TV Report Says U.S. Using Monitoring Posts in China," *Washington Post*, June 18, 1981; and Murrey Marder, "Monitoring: Not-So-Secret Secret," *Washington Post*, June 19, 1981.

During its last months, the Carter administration placed high priority on further institutionalization of economic relations. It also took some steps to try to translate into operational policies the decisions announced during and after Secretary Brown's trip. In September, Under Secretary of Defense for Research and Engineering William J. Perry discussed possible sales of dual-use technology in concrete terms while on a visit to China.[21] In fact, however, there was little concrete follow-through by the U.S. bureaucracies in Washington.

During the initial months of Ronald Reagan's new administration, there was no movement in China policy. As had been the case at the start of the Carter regime, Reagan initially gave China policy low priority. There was widespread uncertainty, in fact, about what Reagan's basic China policy would be (especially toward Taiwan) because of statements he had made during the 1980 campaign that highlighted his strong sympathy toward Taiwan and indicated he would like to upgrade U.S. relations with Taipei (Taibei).

While Reagan's fundamental China policy remained undefined, however, it immediately became clear that his administration was determined to build up U.S. military strength, adopt a harder line toward Moscow, and expand arms sales and other military relationships with countries Washington believed to be opposed to and threatened by the Soviet Union or its proxies. Even before his formal appointment as Reagan's designated secretary of state, General Alexander M. Haig, Jr., strongly emphasized what he called the "strategic" significance of Washington-Beijing ties, asserting that there was an important "compatibility and . . . convergence" in American and Chinese strategic interests.[22]

In May 1981 the Reagan administration announced its first major move in China policy: a trip by Haig to China.[23] In June, just before Haig left for Beijing, the National Security Council decided to take still another major step to try to broaden U.S.-China ties in the military-security field.[24] It was, in the view of many, a logical culmination of the process begun during the

21. Jay Mathews, "U.S. to Let Chinese Buy High-Technology Goods," *Washington Post*, September 11, 1980.

22. "Major Points in the Senate Foreign Relations Committee's Questioning of Haig," *New York Times*, January 11, 1981.

23. "U.S. Announces Haig Will Go to Peking in Late June," *New York Times*, May 14, 1981.

24. See Don Oberdorfer, "U.S. Plans to Sell High-Technology Material to China," *Washington Post*, June 6, 1981; and Don Oberdorfer, "Haig's Asian Venture: From Diplomatic Heights to a Political Downer," *Washington Post*, June 27, 1981.

Carter administration. In a press conference in Beijing, Haig revealed that Washington had decided to remove China from the list of prohibited destinations for munitions control purposes, thus opening up for the first time the possibility of American sales of certain lethal weapons to China (to be decided on a case-by-case basis), though exactly what weapons would be made available remained to be determined.[25] It was apparent that the Reagan administration took this step to reinforce its new worldwide hard-line policy toward Moscow. Haig invited a Chinese military mission (to be headed by Deputy Chief of Staff Liu Huaqing) to come to Washington in the late summer or early fall of 1981 for concrete discussions of possible arms purchases. And following Haig's return home, the U.S. bureaucracy formulated guidelines on what specific weapons would be offered to the Chinese.

This series of U.S. decisions, culminating in mid-1981 in the offer to sell China arms, appeared from the available evidence to be essentially ad hoc. The majority of the decisions were made just before important trips to China by high-level American leaders, and therefore, in a sense, they were "trip-driven" (in the words of a U.S. official directly involved in the process).[26] One major reason for the decisions appeared to be the belief that important new moves to expand U.S.-China ties had to be announced on the occasion of each such trip to keep up the momentum of consolidating the relationship. In addition, since the Chinese clearly hoped to obtain access to Western military technology and equipment, it was believed that loosening the controls restricting China's access to U.S. sources was not only logical but would help to strengthen overall Sino-American relations. (These high-level trips, and the new steps announced on them, were also designed to move the U.S. bureaucracy.)

Chinese Caution and Uncertainty

However, the timing and context of almost all of the decisions highlighted another fact: they were, in a basic sense, symbolic acts. Some appeared to have been made specifically in response to particular Soviet actions (such as the invasion of Afghanistan) and, in the eyes of many observers, the American moves seemed to be aimed at least as much toward

25. Oberdorfer, "Haig's Asian Venture."
26. Private interview with a U.S. official, June 24, 1979; unattributable.

Moscow as toward Beijing. To much of the world, in fact, it appeared that —despite all of Washington's denials—these moves did constitute a manipulative attempt to use the "China card" to try to exert pressure on the Russians.

Despite the Chinese leaders' obvious desire to develop a strategic relationship with Washington and to obtain access to American high technology, it is possible that some of them were uncertain and over time became wary about American motives as a result of the circumstances, timing, and nature of the U.S. decisions. Washington's subsequent slowness in translating the decisions into workable policies must have reinforced their uncertainties. None of the decisions was quickly or effectively implemented by the U.S. bureaucracy.[27] This was in part because of inadequate preparation before the decisions were announced, and in part because policy-related differences and inefficiency resulted in foot-dragging within Washington's bureaucracies.

Some Chinese complained strongly that when they tried to purchase certain authorized items of dual-use technology, they encountered serious obstacles and prolonged delays. They also asserted that many of the items to which they assigned the highest priority continued to be denied to them —including some types of dual-use high technology that clearly were desired for important civilian projects. Others stated privately that, in their opinion, Washington was unlikely to consider authorizing the sale to China of really advanced state-of-the-art weapons (an opinion that doubtless was correct).[28] Actually, as of 1982, the Chinese had purchased virtually none of the military support items that Washington had authorized for sale in 1980.

China's top leaders apparently were more cautious than their American counterparts as they considered the possible long-term implications—including the conceivable quid pro quos that might be involved—if they rushed to accept what the American bearers of gifts offered so dramatically on their visits to Beijing. It was notable that when Secretary Brown, on his

27. See statement of Roger Sullivan in *The Implications of U.S.-China Military Cooperation*, a workshop sponsored by the Senate Committee on Foreign Relations and the Congressional Research Service, Library of Congress, Committee Print, 97 Cong. 1 sess. (GPO, 1981), p. 136. Sullivan, a former National Security Council member who advocated weapons sales to China, states that ever since the U.S. government decided to authorize sales of dual technology and defense-related industrial technology to the Chinese, "the intent of the policy-makers has been effectively thwarted at the working level."

28. Private conversations, February 1982, unattributable.

1980 visit, talked about Washington's desire for "wide cooperation" and "coordinated" action in the security field, the Chinese merely stressed the desirability of taking "parallel" actions and the need for each country to strengthen its "own defense capabilities."[29]

Ever since the 1980 campaign, when Ronald Reagan had called for reestablishing official links with Taiwan, Beijing's leaders had been uncertain and apprehensive about Reagan's basic intentions toward China and Taiwan. In the months prior to Secretary Haig's visit, China's leaders showed steadily increasing concern that Washington was on the verge of selling a new, more sophisticated aircraft to Taiwan (a move that they vehemently opposed), and it was evident that they had become deeply suspicious that Washington might be trying to buy their acquiescence to that move by offering to sell certain weapons to China. Four days *before* Haig's arrival in China—that is, before the Chinese knew that he would announce Washington's decision to sell some arms to Beijing—a spokesman for the Chinese Foreign Ministry stated bluntly: "We would rather receive no U.S. arms than accepting [sic]continued U.S. interference in our internal affairs by selling arms to Taiwan."[30]

American Differences and Doubts

Not only were the Chinese uncertain about the real motives and objectives of U.S. leaders in moving toward concrete military ties and offering arms to China, a good many Americans also raised questions about the basic rationale and objectives of moving toward military relationships with China.

Compared with the years before the Nixon opening, there has been relatively little debate in the United States in recent years about overall China policy. Ever since Nixon's trip, there appears to have been fairly strong and solid public support for the new basic policy of developing friendly political relations with the People's Republic—a fact that is quite remarkable when one recalls that for two and a half decades, from World

29. See the Chinese reports on American and Chinese statements in "Deng Xiaoping Urges Unity against Soviet Global Expansionism," and "Secretary Brown's Visit Important for Contacts between Chinese and U.S. Defense Establishments," press release no. 80/003, Embassy of the People's Republic of China, Washington, D.C., January 16, 1980, pp. 1–4.

30. New China News Agency [hereafter cited as NCNA], June 10, 1981, in FBIS, *Daily Report: PRC*, June 10, 1981, p. B1.

War II until the start of the 1970s, China policy had been one of the most contentious and divisive of all foreign policy issues in the United States.

However, in some respects American opinion has continued to blow hot and cold on China, and attitudes have shifted between euphoria and criticism in response to changing perceptions of developments in China. Moreover, at each major turning point in the development of U.S.-China relations since the early 1970s—for example, when the Shanghai Communiqué was issued in 1972, and when full normalization of relations was agreed upon in late 1978—some Americans, especially those in Congress with strong sympathies for the Nationalist regime, have criticized every U.S.-China compromise on the Taiwan issue. The strongest criticism came in late 1978 and early 1979 when the Carter administration agreed to cut formal diplomatic relations with Taiwan, remove American military forces from the island, and end the U.S. mutual security treaty with the Nationalists—steps that Carter and his advisers had correctly concluded were prerequisites for full diplomatic relations with Beijing.[31] At that time there was widespread concern about the future of Taiwan, even among many Americans who strongly favored full normalization of ties with Beijing, and Congress overwhelmingly supported passage of the Taiwan Relations Act.[32] This legislation went far beyond the steps necessary to continue American relations with the island on a nonofficial basis. It stressed the United States' concern about the island's future security and promised continuing U.S. involvement in Taiwan's defense (through arms sales). Nevertheless, despite the controversies revolving around the Taiwan issue, there is no doubt that the American public at large has supported the steps that have been taken to expand friendly ties with Beijing. In fact, Nixon's China opening and Carter's completion of full normalization of ties with China have been widely regarded as the major foreign policy successes achieved by those two presidents.

However, the strong consensus backing China policy has been based primarily on the perceived benefits of developing political ties and ex-

---

31. For example, Representative Philip M. Crane asserted, "The Carter decision fails every test of an effective and positive foreign policy." Press release, Office of Representative Philip M. Crane, December 16, 1978, p. 1. George P. Bush, formerly U.S. representative to China and subsequently Ronald Reagan's vice-president, declared: "The tragic fact is that the price our government has paid in recognizing the People's Republic of China has not only diminished American credibility in the world but has also darkened the prospects for peace." "Our Deal with Peking: All Cost, No Benefit," *Washington Post*, December 24, 1978.

32. 93 Stat. 14.

panding trade with China. The American public has been poorly informed
and uncertain about the moves to establish military links; there has been
little public debate on the subject. Issues relating to U.S.-China military
relations were seriously debated within the U.S. government bureaucracy,
however. The debates focused especially on how steps toward military links
with China might affect triangular relationships among the United States,
the Soviet Union, and China, and there were significant differences within
the government on this question. Such differences were a major source of
contention, for example, between Secretary of State Vance and national
security adviser Brzezinski, with the former arguing for genuinely evenhanded policies toward Beijing and Moscow and the latter favoring a policy
that would involve a definite pro-Beijing tilt and increasing stress on the
convergence of American and Chinese security interests.[33]

However, no real consensus emerged within the U.S. government on
whether developing significant military relationships with China would be
desirable—and, if so, how and to what extent. Many U.S. officials and
bureaucrats (including some leading China specialists who were among the
strongest advocates of closer political and economic ties with Beijing) had
serious doubts about the wisdom of initiating arms sales to China. When
steps in this direction were taken during 1980–81, some congressmen also
began to express concern about the issue, and during 1981–82 the House
and Senate committees most directly concerned with China policy gave
some attention to the subject.[34] Judging from the public record, however,
there is little basis for believing that there ever was an adequate, system-
atic, comprehensive study of all the possible long-term implications and
consequences of selling arms to China or forging other types of close military relations.

Most U.S. critics of the moves toward military relations between the
United States and China pointed out that such ties could have very significant effects—different from and going beyond the effects of normalized
political and economic ties—on a wide range of other international relationships, including both American and Chinese relations with the Soviet
Union, Japan, Korea, Southeast Asia, and other areas. Even among these

33. See Bernard Gwertzman, "Vance and Brzezinski Differ Again on Peking Tie and
Effect on Soviet," *New York Times*, January 16, 1979.

34. See *The Implications of U.S.-China Military Cooperation*; and *The New Era in East
Asia*, Hearings before the Subcommittee on Asian and Pacific Affairs of the House Committee on Foreign Affairs, 97 Cong. 1 sess. (GPO, 1981).

critics, however, few asked the fundamental question: whether bilateral political relations between the United States and China had been sufficiently consolidated even to consider significant military ties. As soon as Washington made its offer to sell arms to Beijing, it became very clear that they had not.

The Taiwan Time Bomb

When leaders in the Reagan administration decided to authorize arms sales to China, their assumption must have been that security relations were potentially so important to both nations that leaders in both would give lower priority to other concerns, and that an offer of arms to Beijing would itself help to strengthen political ties, overcome Chinese doubts about U.S. intentions, and reduce the political strains in the relationship that had become increasingly apparent during the preceding months. This obviously was a misjudgment.

It was an ironic fact that Beijing refused the Reagan administration's offer of arms before Haig announced it. Following Haig's trip, even though the Chinese initially agreed to send to Washington a military mission headed by Deputy Chief of Staff Liu, they proceeded to escalate their criticism of U.S. policy. Instead of welcoming the arms sales offer, they warned of the possibility of a real crisis over the issue of arms sales to Taiwan, and they indicated quite clearly that if such a crisis occurred it could lead to a downgrading of U.S.-China diplomatic relations.

It has been frequently stated that since the reestablishment of U.S.-China ties in the early 1970s there have been no serious bilateral problems between Washington and Beijing except for those deriving from differences relating to Taiwan. This statement is basically correct, but it is also misleading.

The situation could be described more accurately as follows. Since 1971–72, the United States and China have been remarkably successful in developing a wide variety of important political and economic ties that could provide the basis for a mutually beneficial long-term cooperative relationship, but because of unresolved differences over the Taiwan problem the relationship has remained fundamentally fragile. If the Taiwan problem is not skillfully managed by both sides, it still could at any time not only strain but seriously erode overall Sino-American relations.

Background of the Taiwan Issue

It is not possible here to review in detail the long history of the Taiwan problem as it has affected U.S.-China relations during the years since World War II, but if Americans forget a number of essential facts, the strains in U.S.-China relations over Taiwan are likely to be incomprehensible and unmanageable.[35]

One of these facts is that in a formal sense the civil war between the Chinese Communists and Chinese Nationalists has never been officially ended; leaders in Taipei as well as Beijing still claim to be the government of China. Both officially assert, moreover, that Taiwan is a province of China. China remains, therefore, a divided country. American ties with the Nationalists date back roughly half a century. However, after fighting in the Chinese civil war drew to a close in the late 1940s and the remnants of the defeated Nationalists withdrew to Taiwan, the U.S. government decided in early 1950 to accept the reality of the situation and to disengage from Taiwan. Less than half a year later, however, at the start of the Korean War, the United States reversed itself and reengaged itself in the Chinese civil war, and soon thereafter Washington resumed aid to the Nationalist regime. In 1954 Washington signed an open-ended mutual security treaty with Taipei. As a result of these developments, the United States continued for almost three decades to recognize the Nationalist government in Taipei as the government of China, to pursue a policy of nonrecognition toward the People's Republic, and to be the principal supporter of a regime that officially continued to challenge Beijing's claim to be China's sole legal government.[36]

Gradually, the Nationalists on Taiwan developed a relatively stable local political regime and one of the most dynamic and successful economies in Asia. Over time, Taipei's claim to be the government of China lost all credibility, and international recognition of it as the government of China steadily eroded. Nevertheless, the Nationalist leaders, with American support, successfully operated a de facto separate regime, and the prospects for reunification of China appeared to decline steadily.

The leaders in Taipei have consistently refused to consider any steps toward reunification—or even the establishment of any direct contacts with

35. For background, see Ralph N. Clough, *Island China* (Harvard University Press, 1978).

36. For data on Taiwan and U.S. and Chinese policy relating to it in the 1950s, see A. Doak Barnett, *Communist China and Asia: Challenge to American Policy* (Harper for the Council on Foreign Relations, 1960).

Beijing. The population of the island, moreover, has remained staunchly anti-Communist and opposed to the idea of accepting control by Beijing. Probably many, even among the mainlanders who came to the island in the late 1940s, would now opt if they could for long-term separation from China. Many local Taiwanese, whose ancestors migrated from China centuries ago, would doubtless opt for formal independence if they were given the choice and if they believed that an independent Taiwan would be viable. Most recognize, however, that this is unlikely to be a feasible option in the foreseeable future, and therefore many—perhaps a majority—tend to favor continuation of Taiwan's present de facto status, while hoping that eventually local political control will shift from the hands of the mainlanders, who still dominate the regime, to local Taiwanese, who make up the bulk of the population.

Taiwan could not have maintained its separate status during the past three decades or achieved the degree of political stability or the kind of economic success that it has without major U.S. political, military, and economic support, as well as close economic links with Japan. While the island gradually has developed considerable independent economic strength, it remains highly dependent on its trade and other economic relations with these two powers. Even though both Japan and the United States have severed formal diplomatic relations with Taipei (Japan in 1972 and the United States in 1979), both have continued, with Beijing's acquiescence, to maintain important nonofficial political ties and broadly based economic relations with Taiwan. And the United States has continued to provide Taiwan with weapons for its armed forces.

China's Reunification Strategy

Beijing's leaders, however, have never abandoned their aim of reunifying the country. They have strongly felt (as the Nationalist leaders doubtless would have, too, if they had won the Chinese civil war) that as long as Taiwan remains separate, China's unification—a fundamental national goal—is incomplete. They also believe, with some justification, that in many respects the United States has been responsible for the prolonged separation of Taiwan from the mainland. They always have maintained that U.S. ties with Taiwan, in particular diplomatic and military ties, have represented illegitimate intervention in China's domestic affairs.

The actual priority that Beijing has given to the goal of reunification has changed several times over the years, however, as international circumstances have changed, and its strategy to work toward reunification has varied greatly in different periods. In late 1949 and early 1950, China's People's Liberation Army actively prepared to invade Taiwan, as it earlier had invaded Hainan, China's other major offshore island, and, if the United States had not reintervened in mid-1950, the PLA doubtless would have attempted it. (Despite the difficulty of the task, the invasion probably would have succeeded, because of the demoralization of the Nationalist regime and its military forces at that time.) Then the U.S. decision in mid-1950 to interpose the Seventh Fleet in the Taiwan Strait to prevent any invasion effectively blocked this possibility.

Thereafter, following the Korean War, Beijing renewed its attempts to work toward reunification through a combination of military pressure and negotiations. Its two major efforts to use military pressure were in 1954–55 and 1958. In both cases Beijing initiated local crises by intense bombardment of the Nationalist-held offshore islands, located near the mainland coast opposite Taiwan (where the Nationalists maintained some of their best military forces). The available evidence suggests that in neither case did Beijing intend to invade Taiwan itself; it lacked the military capability to do so. In both cases, its primary aim apparently was to try to demoralize the Nationalists, convince Washington that it should disengage from the area, and induce Taiwan to submit to or accommodate with Beijing.

The offshore islands crises failed to achieve these objectives; instead, they resulted in stronger U.S. support of the Nationalist regime. It is true that they did lead the United States to "leash" the Nationalists—to impose restrictions designed to prevent them from initiating military actions against the mainland that could have created crises involving the United States. However, from Beijing's perspective, this was at best a mixed blessing; at worst, it was a net loss, since it appeared to support trends toward a permanent two-Chinas situation. Since 1958, there has been no indication that Beijing's leaders have seriously considered using intensive military pressure to try to "liberate" Taiwan.

China's attempt to negotiate a solution started when it opened talks with the United States at Geneva in the mid-1950s. Although these negotiations (later continued at Warsaw) were not just about Taiwan, it was always the central issue. Beijing's aim was to obtain U.S. acceptance of its sovereignty over the island (as well as acceptance of the mainland regime as China's sole legal government), and ultimately to induce the Americans to disengage from Taiwan. However, the primary aim of Washington was to induce Beijing to renounce the use of force against the island; this Beijing consistently refused to do since, in its view, such a move would have compromised its sovereignty. Although these Sino-American talks continued until the late 1960s, they were basically sterile and produced no agreement on any of the key issues.[37]

In that period, Beijing supplemented its military pressures and its negotiations with the Americans with some steps—directed at both the mainlander Nationalist leaders and local Taiwanese—to try to pursue a policy of attraction. In the mid-1950s it proposed direct negotiations with the Nationalist leaders and offered them posts in Beijing, but this evoked no positive response. It also organized a Taiwan Democratic Self-Government League, but this was totally ineffectual.

All of these efforts in the 1950s failed, and by the 1960s Beijing appeared to have no real strategy for reunification that had any prospects for success. It continued to call (sometimes threateningly) for "liberation" of the island, and there was ample evidence that Chinese concern about a permanent two-Chinas situation steadily increased. However, until 1968, Chinese leaders appeared to have few new ideas on how to approach the Taiwan problem. In practical terms, Taiwan appeared almost to drop off Beijing's priority policy agenda. Moreover, the Chinese were heavily preoccupied at that time with other problems—in foreign policy with the Sino-Soviet conflict and the Vietnamese war, and at home with the Cultural Revolution.

In late 1968, however, Beijing signaled its desire for renewed talks with the United States, and soon after Richard M. Nixon's inauguration in 1969, he and Henry Kissinger began signaling the American desire for high-level talks.

Limited Compromise on Taiwan

Inevitably, Taiwan came to the fore again when China and the United States decided to explore the possibilities of moving toward détente in the early 1970s. Leaders in both countries recognized that détente would not be possible without some compromise on the Taiwan issue, which had been the principal obstacle to any ties between them ever since 1950. Ultimately they found that some compromises were possible.

The first compromises, in the carefully crafted Shanghai Communiqué

37. See Kenneth T. Young, *Negotiating With The Chinese Communists: The United States Experience, 1953-1967* (McGraw-Hill for the Council on Foreign Relations, 1968).

of 1972, were limited. The Chinese stood absolutely firm on what they regarded as fundamental principles, but they decided to be more pragmatic and to proceed with the establishment of nonofficial contacts with the United States even though the basic problem remained unresolved. (For some years, they had asserted strongly that the Taiwan problem had to be solved *before* even nonofficial U.S.-China relations could be developed.)

In the communiqué, the Chinese reaffirmed their position that the People's Republic is the sole legal government of China, that Taiwan is a Chinese province, and that the liberation of the island is an internal affair. They also asserted that all U.S. military forces must be removed from Taiwan.

The United States, on its part, made a cautious move in the direction of accepting Beijing's claims by "acknowledging that all Chinese on either side of the Taiwan Strait maintain that there is but one China and that Taiwan is a part of China," adding that Washington "does not challenge that position." But it did not explicitly recognize Chinese sovereignty over Taiwan. Washington also reaffirmed its "interest in a peaceful settlement of the Taiwan question by the Chinese themselves," and stated that, "with that prospect in mind," the United States "affirms the ultimate objective of the withdrawal of all U.S. forces" from the island and would "progressively reduce them . . . as the tension in the area diminishes."[38] However, Washington continued its recognition of, and defense treaty with, the Nationalist regime. This very limited compromise in effect deferred any attempt to agree on the key issues, but under the circumstances it was sufficient to permit the initiation of nonofficial U.S.-China ties.

The compromises required for full normalization, roughly seven years later, were much more substantial. In certain respects, Washington made the most important and obvious concessions. The United States now recognized that the People's Republic of China is the sole legal government of China, and stated that Washington "acknowledges the Chinese position that there is but one China and Taiwan is part of China."[39] (This, too, fell short of explicit U.S. recognition that Taiwan is a Chinese province legally belonging to the People's Republic, but the Chinese doubtless viewed it as another step in that direction.) Most important, Washington agreed to

38. See the text in *Department of State Bulletin*, vol. 66, no. 1708 (March 20, 1972), pp. 435–38.

39. See the text in "Normalization of Relations With the People's Republic of China," news release, Department of State, Bureau of Public Affairs, Office of Public Communication, December 15, 1978, p. 1.

terminate formal diplomatic relations with the Nationalist regime, end its defense treaty with it, and withdraw all U.S. forces from the island. However, at the same time the United States stated, with Beijing's acquiescence, that it would "maintain commercial, cultural, and other [unofficial] relations" with Taiwan, and declared that it "expects that the Taiwan issue will be settled peacefully by the Chinese themselves."[40]

During the negotiations leading to normalization Washington also made it very clear to the Chinese that it intended to continue to sell defensive arms to Taiwan, and, although Beijing regarded this as illegitimate and highly objectionable, it decided nevertheless to proceed with full normalization of relations.[41] The issue of U.S. arms sales to Taiwan was the crucial one in the negotiations. Beijing's decision not to force the issue at that time was doubtless highly controversial in China, and it represented a much greater concession than most Americans recognized.

The agreement on normalization therefore required major and difficult concessions by both sides. While the Chinese obtained from Washington most of the major concessions on principles, it can be argued that they made some of the most important concessions in practical, substantive terms. Not only did they agree to the continuation of U.S. economic and other relationships with Taiwan on a nonofficial basis (as they already had agreed Japan could do when Sino-Japanese relations were normalized in 1972), they tacitly acquiesced to the U.S. insistence on continuing arms sales to Taiwan.

It is not correct, however, to say—as many observers have—that Beijing "agreed to disagree" on this. At the time of normalization, Hua Guofeng (then party chairman) publicly stated Beijing's official position on U.S. arms sales to Taiwan: "We absolutely would not agree to this."[42] What the Chinese did was tacitly agree to defer the issue by proceeding to normalize relations even though they knew the Americans intended to continue such arms sales. It was predictable that at some point the Chinese would raise this issue again and press the United States to end all arms sales to Taiwan. The question was when—and few Americans tried to predict the answer or

40. Ibid., p. 2.

41. "Diplomatic Relations With the People's Republic of China and Future Relations With Taiwan," news release, Department of State, Bureau of Public Affairs, Office of Public Communication, December 1978, p. 2.

42. "Chairman Hua Gives Press Conference," *Peking Review*, no. 51 (December 22, 1978), p. 10. The Chinese Liaison Office in Washington, D.C., quoted Hua as saying: "We can absolutely not agree to this"; see press release, Liaison Office, People's Republic of China, Washington, D.C., December 1978.

to think ahead about how to handle the issue in the future. It is conceivable that few Chinese did, either.

Chinese and American Expectations

It is extremely difficult to know exactly what the real expectations and hopes of both the American and Chinese leaders were when they decided on the compromises necessary to proceed with normalization. It is almost certain, however, that they were far from identical.

Most of the Americans involved in the process of normalization fully recognized that the Taiwan problem had not been permanently solved, and that it would arise again as an issue sometime in the future. Yet most appeared to hope—and some seemed to expect—that Beijing would be able to live with the existing de facto situation, including continued U.S. arms sales to Taiwan, for a prolonged period of time, perhaps for the indefinite future. It was believed that if normalization led to the creation of expanding U.S.-China political, economic, and security ties of increasing mutual benefit, then perhaps the Taiwan problem could be gradually defused. Eventually, it was hoped, some kind of "peaceful" solution would become possible, though few American officials were confident in speculating about what kind of solution ultimately might prove to be feasible or desirable or how it might evolve.

It is possible that some Chinese leaders shared the hope or expectation that the Taiwan problem could be removed as an obstacle to closer U.S.-China relations for a prolonged period of time. Certain leaders, including Deng Xiaoping (as well as Mao Zedong before him), periodically had made statements indicating that the Chinese would be patient in approaching the problem of reunification and recognized that a solution might require decades.[43] Yet there also is reason to believe that at least certain Chinese leaders viewed the problem with greater urgency and feared that continuation of the existing de facto situation could lead to the permanent separation of Taiwan rather than to reunification.

Some Chinese leaders may well have opposed or at least have been skeptical about the wisdom of acquiescing to continued U.S. arms sales to Taiwan. Moreover, it is probable that virtually all leaders in Beijing (in-

43. See, for example, Deng's statement quoted in Frank S. T. Hsiao and Lawrence R. Sullivan, "The Politics of Reunification: Beijing's Initiative on Taiwan," *Asian Survey*, vol. 20 (August 1980), p. 790.

cluding Deng, who played a key personal role in the normalization process and doubtless was regarded by many in China as being ultimately responsible for the decision to defer the Taiwan arms sale issue) at least hoped that after normalization (and after the one-year moratorium on such sales promised by U.S. leaders) Washington would exercise increased restraint in arms sales to Taiwan and gradually reduce its military ties with the island. If this occurred, the Chinese leaders hoped, the political effect of normalization would be to create a new climate in the area that would gradually exert pressure on Taiwan's leaders to open a dialogue with Beijing.

Peaceful Reunification Campaign

On January 1, 1979, the day that diplomatic ties between the United States and China were formally established, Beijing launched a major new campaign for peaceful reunification. The Standing Committee of China's National People's Congress, in a "Message to Compatriots in Taiwan," announced the end of all bombardment of the offshore islands (which by this time was sporadic and symbolic), called for peaceful reunification, and proposed "discussion between the Government of the People's Republic of China and the Taiwan authorities." It talked of the "necessary prerequisites" for ending "military confrontation" and creating "a secure environment for the two sides to make contacts and exchanges," and it proposed steps "at an early date" to start direct trade, transportation, and postal services, and to encourage two-way tours and visits and "academic, cultural, sports, and technological interchanges."[44]

This proposal was not totally lacking precedents. As noted earlier, in the mid-1950s Beijing had proposed direct negotiations with Taiwan. And for some time certain Chinese leaders had shown increasing flexibility and moderation in discussing the Taiwan problem. Nevertheless, the NPC's statement clearly launched a new strategy that was more pragmatic and conciliatory than any in the past. Asserting that Beijing would "take present realities into account" in the process of reunification, it promised that China would "respect the status quo on Taiwan" and "adopt reasonable policies and measures ... so as not to cause the people of Taiwan any

44. "Message to Compatriots in Taiwan," *Beijing Review*, no. 1 (January 5, 1979), p. 17.

losses."[45] The statement lacked any real specifics, however, and to no one's surprise Taipei's leaders rejected Beijing's overtures.

Both before and following this statement, Chinese officials and Beijing's press actually went further than the NPC statement did. In a variety of statements, the Chinese indicated that they would not "change the society [on Taiwan] by force," and would allow the island to "maintain its present economic and social systems."[46] Yet Beijing remained vague on exactly what kind of status Taiwan might have after reunification.

Although the January 1, 1979, statement spoke of Beijing's desire to achieve reunification at an "early date," it is debatable whether many Chinese leaders actually expected rapid progress toward that goal. It is likely, however, that they hoped that their unprecedented conciliatory stance—announced when Washington-Beijing ties were normalized and the United States ended formal diplomatic links with Taipei—would lead soon to some direct China-Taiwan contacts that could help to lay the basis for eventual negotiations.

Beijing's leaders probably hoped that at the very minimum their new strategy toward Taiwan, plus normalized U.S.-China relations, would halt what they had long perceived as a steady drift toward the permanent separation of Taiwan. They must also have hoped that the increased priority that Washington now appeared to give to its relations with China would at least indirectly exert an influence on Taiwan's leaders that would increase the chance of some sort of dialogue between Beijing and Taipei.

The January 1 statement was followed by a number of concrete unilateral actions by Beijing to try to expand contacts. Significant steps were taken to encourage trade, such as ending customs duties on goods from Taiwan. Beijing strongly urged Taiwanese businessmen to consider involvement in cooperative economic projects in China, especially in China's new special economic zones (including one established at Xiamen [Amoy], on the Fujian coast opposite Taiwan). It also encouraged scholars, students, and others from China to meet with counterparts from Taiwan in third countries. Many invitations were sent by various organizations in China to people of all kinds on Taiwan to make visits to the mainland. And Beijing indicated its willingness to have two Chinese Olympics teams if Taiwan participants did not use the Republic of China's name or flag.

It should be noted that even though leaders in Taipei officially denounced Beijing's new strategy and vowed that they would never enter into

45. Ibid.
46. Hsiao and Sullivan, "The Politics of Reunification," p. 792.

negotiations with the People's Republic, in practice they too gradually began to show some signs of increased flexibility. Not only did they start to encourage some nonofficial contacts in third countries; most important, they tolerated a rapid growth of indirect trade—largely through Hong Kong—which by 1982 amounted to several hundred million dollars annually.

Seeds of Doubt in Beijing

In general, Beijing's leaders still appeared willing during 1979–80 to take a fairly long-range gradual approach to developing contacts and a dialogue with Taiwan. They seemed prepared to allow considerable time to test whether their conciliatory policy of attraction would gradually have the desired political effects, and whether the United States would gradually reduce its military ties with the Nationalists and its arms sales to the island.

Within months of the agreement on normalizing U.S.-China ties, however, leaders in Beijing had reason to question whether postnormalization U.S. policy would, in fact, support China's new strategy of peaceful reunification. A large number of U.S. congressmen, including many who favored normalization of relations with Beijing, criticized the way in which normalization had been carried out. Believing that the Carter administration had not dealt adequately with the question of U.S. concern for Taiwan's future security, they rapidly drafted and passed the Taiwan Relations Act. Chinese leaders probably were genuinely shocked by the scope and form of the policy statements embodied in this act, and they strongly protested its passage.

The act not only stated that the U.S. decision to normalize relations with Beijing "rests upon the expectation that the future of Taiwan will be determined by peaceful means" (which was similar to many previous U.S. statements), it asserted that any effort to determine the island's future "by other than peaceful means, including by boycotts or embargoes" would be considered "a threat to the peace and security of the Western Pacific area and of grave concern to the United States." It declared formally that Washington would make available to Taiwan "arms of a defensive character," stating that the president and Congress would determine "the character and quantity" that Taiwan "needs." And it asserted that the United States itself should "maintain the capacity . . . to resist any resort to force or other forms of coercion" threatening to Taiwan's security or its "social or economic system."[47] The Chinese probably had expected the Americans to deal with these controversial issues in a more low-key, subtle fashion, less blatantly challenging to Chinese claims of sovereignty, and they viewed the act as a new kind of unilateral U.S. defense commitment to Taiwan that in some respects went further and was even broader than the mutual security treaty that Congress designed it to replace.[48]

President Carter tried to reassure the Chinese about his administration's intentions when he signed the Taiwan Relations Act by stressing that as president he had discretion regarding how to implement the act. He promised to "exercise that discretion in a manner consistent with our interest, in the well-being of the people on Taiwan, and with the understandings we reached on the normalization of relations."[49]

However, the U.S. government's subsequent actions, during even the Carter administration, were far from reassuring to Beijing. Despite Washington's promise of a formal one-year moratorium on new arms sales contracts with Taiwan, actual arms deliveries continued at a substantial level, and when new sales resumed they were unexpectedly large. Beijing probably expected a drop in U.S. arms sales to Taiwan following U.S.-China normalization. In fact, U.S. Foreign Military Sales (FMS) to the island actually exceeded a half billion dollars a year in both fiscal 1979 and fiscal 1980.[50]

In mid-1980 Carter authorized U.S. aircraft manufacturers to discuss possible sales of a more advanced aircraft, the so-called FX (either the F-5G or F-16/79), to a number of possible foreign buyers, including the government on Taiwan.[51] The Chinese press immediately and strongly criticized this as "a breach of the principles stipulated in the agreement on the

47. Public Law 96-8, 193 Stat. 14; text in Richard H. Solomon, ed., *The China Factor: Sino-American Relations and the Global Scene* (Prentice-Hall, 1981), pp. 304–14.

48. The fact that the act was broader than the security treaty in some respects in its assurances regarding Taiwan's security was pointed out by prominent scholars on Taiwan; see King-yuh Chang, "Partnership in Transition: A Review of Recent Taipei-Washington Relations," *Asian Survey*, vol. 21 (June 1981), pp. 608, 609. (The author was deputy director of the Institute of International Affairs in Taiwan.)

49. See the president's statement in "East Asia: Taiwan Relations Act," *Department of State Bulletin*, vol. 79, no. 2027 (June 1979), p. 26.

50. Security Assistance Agency, Department of Defense, *Foreign Military Sales and Military Assistance Facts, December 1980* (Data Management Division, Comptroller, DSAA, December 1980), p. 2.

51. "U.S. to Let Firms Discuss Sale of FX Jet to Taiwan," *Washington Post*, June 13, 1980.

establishment of diplomatic relations between China and the United States which . . . jeopardized China's cause for the return of Taiwan."52

Even if Carter had been elected to a second term, the Taiwan arms sales issue might have gradually escalated and perhaps fairly soon become a serious issue in U.S.-China relations. However, during Carter's final year in office, his administration took a series of constructive steps to strengthen political and economic ties between Washington and Beijing. While the Chinese clearly were disturbed by the trend in U.S. arms sales to Taiwan, as well as by the Taiwan Relations Act, they generally emphasized the positive as U.S.-China relations steadily expanded. Whatever the reasons, they did not then press hard on Taiwan-related questions.

Nevertheless, there already were signs suggesting that postnormalization U.S. policy on Taiwan had revived debate within China on what effects normalization would have on Beijing's reunification strategy. Even Deng began to show some signs of impatience, perhaps as a result of pressure and criticism from others in the Chinese leadership. At about the same time that the Taiwan Relations Act was signed, Deng reminded the world that if Taiwan persistently refused even to start talks, China retained the right to consider the use of force to unify the country.53 And in a speech in January 1980 outlining China's major tasks in the decade ahead, Deng listed reunification as one of three goals that should have highest priority (though the way in which he discussed the three suggested that he, at least, still regarded the Taiwan issue as third in priority, behind domestic modernization and opposition to Soviet hegemonism).54

Gradually, from the middle of 1980 on, it became increasingly evident that Beijing was more and more concerned about what future U.S. policy toward Taiwan would be. In particular, statements made by presidential candidate Ronald Reagan created great apprehension in Beijing. During his campaign, Reagan stated, first, that he favored restoring "official relations" with Taiwan, then (retreating somewhat), that he intended at least to establish an official liaison office in Taiwan, and finally (retreating still further), that at a minimum he "would not pretend . . . that the relationship we now have with Taiwan, enacted by our Congress, is not official."55

From the time that Reagan began making such statements, the Chinese

52. NCNA report in FBIS, *Daily Report: PRC*, June 23, 1980, p. B1.

53. Hsiao and Sullivan, "The Politics of Reunification," pp. 796–97.

54. "Text of Deng Xiaoping's Report on the Current Situation and Tasks," in FBIS, *Daily Report: PRC*, Supplement, March 11, 1980, pp. 1–27.

55. See Don Oberdorfer, "Reagan Mired in Touchy China Dispute," *Washington Post*, August 20, 1980; Howell Raines, "Reagan, Conceding Misstatements, Abandons Plans on

bitterly attacked them, and also increased criticism of all U.S. arms sales to Taiwan. On the urging of many of his advisers, Reagan steadily back-tracked, and both he and his advisers tried to reassure Beijing that he believed U.S.-China relations to be important. He even sent his vice-presidential running mate, George Bush, to China to explain his views, but Bush was unable to mollify the Chinese. They were aware not only that Reagan himself had strong personal sympathies for Taiwan but also that some of his close advisers had long had important ties with Taipei.

During the year following Reagan's election, the Chinese greatly esca-lated their criticism of U.S. policy toward Taiwan and increasingly articu-lated in public suspicions about basic U.S. government motives and inten-tions regarding China. Clearly, the confidence of Chinese leaders in U.S. policy toward Taiwan and China was seriously weakened, starting in mid-1980. Since early 1981 Reagan and Secretary of State Haig have tried to reestablish mutual confidence in the U.S.-China relationship, but as of early 1982 they had not been successful.

The FX Issue

Throughout much of 1981 the main focus of Chinese political attacks appeared to be the possible sale of the FX to Taiwan, but their underlying concerns obviously were much broader; the FX served as a symbol for these broader concerns.[56] Both before and after Haig's visit to Beijing in mid-1981, instead of expressing satisfaction about the fact that the Reagan administration now stressed the strategic importance of U.S.-China ties and appeared willing to authorize arms sales to China, the Chinese became increasingly shrill, and in numerous articles and commentaries they repeat-edly impugned the Reagan administration's fundamental motives. Bei-jing's press openly charged that Washington was "engaged in the creation of 'two Chinas' " and was attempting to do so by a devious approach—"to sell arms to China in exchange for China's consent to U.S. arms sales to Taiwan." It accused Washington of following an arrogant "superpower

---

Taiwan Office," *New York Times*, August 26, 1980; and Howell Raines, "Reagan Denies Plan to Answer Carter," *New York Times*, August 17, 1980.

56. On the controversy over the FX, see A. Doak Barnett, *The FX Decision: "Another Crucial Moment" in U.S.-China Relations* (Brookings Institution, 1981).

logic," asserting that "in the eyes of a superpower, it is in its interest if a country or nation is split into two parts by outside intervention."[57]

The United States, the Chinese press charged, seems to believe that "as China is in need of American support on the question of combatting Soviet hegemonism, it will have to swallow the 'bitter pill' " of whatever Taiwan policy U.S. leaders might choose to follow. The Chinese warned that they never would accept such "bullying" and pointedly drew a parallel with the causes of the Sino-Soviet split. "In the 1960s, under extremely difficult conditions," said a commentator, "China waged a resolute struggle against the oppression and bullying by the Soviet hegemonists in order to defend the principles of independence, sovereignty, and equality, not hesitating to bear the consequence of a break with the Soviet Union."[58] The Chinese clearly implied that, if Washington decided to sell the FX to Taiwan, Beijing would downgrade diplomatic relations with the United States, just as it had done with the Netherlands in early 1981 when the Dutch sold two advanced submarines to Taiwan.

Beijing also warned the Americans not to think that the Chinese would have to accept whatever decisions Washington might make on arms sales to Taiwan because China needed economic as well as strategic support from the Americans. "In the United States there are still some people," one strong Chinese article asserted, "who . . . absurdly say that as China has to rely on the United States to cope with the Soviet threat and that China needs U.S. assistance to realize its four modernizations," Beijing will have to accept any U.S. policy toward Taiwan.[59] Another harsh article declared that the Chinese people "may have weaknesses of one kind or another, but they surely will not be lackeys to any foreign country and bow to any superpower."[60]

By the late summer of 1981, it was virtually certain that, if Washington decided to sell the FX to Taiwan, Beijing would downgrade U.S.-China official relations. While no decision had yet been made on this specific issue in Washington, the continued delay in making a decision simply reinforced Chinese suspicions. The decision obviously was not an easy one for Reagan

57. Hua Xiu, "A Move Doomed to Failure," NCNA, June 11, 1981, in FBIS, *Daily Report: PRC,* June 12, 1981, p. B1.

58. "Commentary: A Key Link in Development of Sino-U.S. Relations," NCNA, June 18, 1981, in FBIS, *Daily Report: PRC,* June 19, 1981, p. B2.

59. Zhuang Qubing, Zhang Hongzeng, and Pan Tongwen, "On the U.S. 'Taiwan Relations Act,' " *Beijing Review,* no. 37 (September 14, 1981), p. 24.

60. Peng Di, "Commentary: A Fantasy to Apply U.S. Law in China," NCNA, August 26, 1981, in FBIS, *Daily Report: PRC,* August 27, 1981, p. B2.

to make. However, Secretary Haig, who late in the year publicly called the issue a "very worrisome specter" that had to be handled with great "sensitivity and care,"[61] argued strongly against the FX sale, and a decision finally was reached *not* to make it. At the same time, however, the administration decided to permit arrangements for continued coproduction in Taiwan of the F-5E.

In late December 1981 Washington announced that it had approved a sizable new sale of military spare parts to Taiwan.[62] In early January 1982 Assistant Secretary of State John H. Holdridge was sent to Beijing to inform the Chinese about the decision not to sell the FX but to continue coproducing the F-5E on Taiwan.[63]

Clearly, the Reagan administration considered its decision against the FX sale to be a significant concession to China, and it is conceivable that if this decision had been announced months earlier it might have forestalled the Chinese decision to broaden the issue and increase pressure on Washington. However, by the time Washington reached a decision, Chinese leaders had broadened the issue, and they made it clear that they were not satisfied.

Pressure to Limit All Arms Sales

When the decision to sell spare parts to Taiwan was announced, the Chinese press strongly denounced it. Shortly thereafter, when Holdridge informed them about the decisions on the FX and F-5E, the Chinese Foreign Ministry officially protested, stating that China "will never accept" any "unilateral" decision by the Americans. It declared, "The whole question of United States arms sales to Taiwan is a major issue affecting China's sovereignty, which must be settled through discussions between the United States and Chinese governments."[64]

U.S. leaders obviously had hoped that the FX decision would reduce the level of tensions over the general issue of arms sales to Taiwan. Instead,

61. Bernard Gwertzman, "Haig Sees Trouble in Ties With China Over Taiwan Arms," *New York Times*, November 15, 1981.

62. Don Oberdorfer, "Spare Part Sale to Taiwan Approved," *Washington Post*, December 29, 1981.

63. Richard Halloran, "U.S. to Let Taiwan Buy Some Jets But Not More Advanced Fighters," *New York Times*, January 12, 1982.

64. Christopher S. Wren, "Peking Protests Sale of U.S. Planes to Taiwan," *New York Times*, January 13, 1982.

tensions immediately rose still higher. Soon after Holdridge's visit, Vice Foreign Minister Zhong Xidong stated bluntly in an interview: "It is no exaggeration to say that [U.S.-China] relations are now at crisis"; there is "practically no room for maneuver on the part of China."[65]

During much of 1981, although the Chinese criticized all sales of U.S. arms to Taiwan, their primary concern seemed to focus on the FX. However, it appears appears that sometime in the late summer or early fall of 1981 China's leaders decided to broaden the issue, increase pressure on Washington, and demand that the United States set qualitative, quantitative, and time limits on *all* arms sales to Taiwan. The Chinese began to press hard for Washington to indicate more explicitly than in the past that the United States accepts Beijing's sovereignty over Taiwan, acknowledges that "in principle" it is unjustifiable to sell arms to a Chinese province, and commits itself not only to reduce all arms sales to Taiwan but also to set a time when such sales will be totally ended.

The fact that Beijing had "raised the ante" in regard to the Taiwan arms sales issue began to be clear when Premier Zhao Ziyang met President Reagan at Cancún, Mexico, in October, and when Foreign Minister Huang Hua met President Reagan and Secretary of State Haig in Washington shortly thereafter.[66] Not only did the Chinese press continue to denounce vehemently all U.S. arms sales to Taiwan, Beijing's leaders privately began pushing for some sort of U.S. commitment to set limits on such sales. The Chinese indicated that they would insist that the U.S. and Chinese governments discuss the issue and work out some sort of understanding or agreement about it. By this time, American officials concluded that they had no alternative but to enter into official discussions on the broad issue of arms sales to Taiwan unless they were prepared to see Beijing downgrade official relations. Talks began in the fall, and, following Holdridge's visit, there were very intensive discussions on the subject. Though the talks were secret, there were many indications that they were extremely difficult, and there was great uncertainty about what the outcome would be.

China's Stepped-Up Reunification Campaign

When China began to increase its pressure on Washington to agree to limit U.S. arms sales to Taiwan, it also intensified its political campaign for

65. Reuter report in FBIS, *Daily Report: PRC*, February 8, 1982, p. B2.
66. See "Reagan Meets the Third World," *Newsweek*, November 2, 1981, pp. 34–35; and NCNA report, October 31, 1981, in FBIS, *Daily Report: PRC*, November 2, 1981, p. B1.

peaceful reunification. This was more than a coincidence. The new moves in the reunification campaign were obviously directed not only toward Taiwan but toward the United States as well. They were intended to convince both Taipei and Washington that Beijing was serious about initiating a political dialogue with Taipei and was prepared to consider fairly far-reaching concessions in order to move toward reunification. They also were designed to counter the arguments of those who maintained that U.S. arms sales to Taiwan were essential because the island faced a potential military threat from China.

Beijing organized a highly publicized celebration on the Nationalists' "national day" (October 10) to glorify Sun Yat-sen, founder of the Kuomintang (Guomindang), and invited Chinese from all over the world to attend.[67] More important, shortly before that celebration, on September 30 (the eve of Beijing's own "national day"), Ye Jianying, chairman of the Standing Committee of China's National People's Congress, issued another major statement on Beijing's policy on peaceful reunification.

This statement went further, was more conciliatory, and offered more specific concessions to Taiwan than any previous statement made by Beijing. In fact, one might argue that it went about as far as any Chinese government conceivably could go in attempting to demonstrate flexibility and make verbal assurances to leaders on Taiwan.

The statement called for reunification "talks" on a "reciprocal basis" and suggested that to lay the foundation for such talks the "two sides may first send people to meet for an exhaustive exchange of views." Ye proposed that as soon as possible there be an agreement "to facilitate the exchange of mails, trade, air and shipping services, family reunions and visits by relatives and tourists as well as academic, cultural, and sports exchanges." He also suggested that even before reunification people on Taiwan should feel free "to make proposals and suggestions regarding affairs of state through various channels and in various ways."

Ye promised that after reunification "Taiwan can enjoy a high degree of autonomy as a special administrative region and it can retain its armed forces," adding that the "central government will not interfere with local affairs on Taiwan." He declared that "Taiwan's current socio-economic system will remain unchanged, so will its way of life and its economic and cultural relations with foreign countries." He also promised that there

67. "Revolution of 1911 Commemorated," *Beijing Review*, no. 42 (October 19, 1981), pp. 5–6.

would be no encroachment on private property rights or foreign investments in Taiwan.

Ye said that Beijing would like for "people in authority and representative personages" from Taiwan to accept "posts of leadership in national political bodies" in Beijing, and he welcomed people from Taiwan to settle on the mainland, promising that they would have "freedom of entry and exit." Finally, he urged "industrialists and businessmen in Taiwan" to "invest and engage in various economic undertakings on the mainland," asserting that "their legal rights, interest, and profits" would be "guaranteed."[68]

Despite the specifics contained in Ye's statement, however, it obviously left a large number of major questions unanswered. It said nothing about how Taiwan could retain its armed forces in any meaningful sense if it could not purchase arms from abroad. An official Chinese journal shortly afterward indicated that ultimately Beijing would control the supply of arms to Taiwan. "As for the replacement of weapons by the armed forces in Taiwan," it said, "arrangements will be made by the central government after reunification according to an overall plan."[69] Ye did not clarify how Taiwan's "high degree of autonomy as a special administrative region" would differ in reality from the so-called autonomy of regions such as Tibet, which in fact have been strictly controlled from Beijing. His offer of "posts of leadership in national political bodies" contained no specifics to reassure those who assumed that at best such posts would be no more than powerless sinecures such as those given to some non-Communists in Beijing's government in earlier years. And while he assured Taiwan that it could continue to maintain nonofficial foreign ties, his statement clearly implied that all of Taiwan's remaining official ties abroad would have to end.

Nevertheless, Ye's statement was important, and even Secretary Haig publicly called it "rather remarkable."[70] Being realists, Beijing's leaders doubtless had no illusions that any statement by them, no matter how conciliatory, could suddenly change basic attitudes on Taiwan and rapidly lead to actual negotiations with Taipei. Predictably, Taipei promptly denounced and rejected Beijing's proposals. However, Chinese leaders proba-

68. "Chairman Ye Jianying's Elaborations on Policy Concerning Return of Taiwan to Motherland and Peaceful Reunification," *Beijing Review*, no. 40 (October 5, 1981), pp. 10–11.

69. "Sales of Weapons to Taiwan," *Beijing Review*, no. 44 (November 2, 1981), p. 3.

70. Bernard Gwertzman, "Haig Sees Trouble in Ties With China Over Taiwan Arms."

bly did hope that their new stance would help to create a political climate that gradually would improve the prospects for China-Taiwan contacts and lead ultimately to a genuine dialogue, and that adoption of a moderate stance also would reinforce their increasing pressure on the United States to agree to restrict, and ultimately end, arms sales to Taiwan.

China's Goals in Negotiations

When discussions on the Taiwan arms sales issue got under way, it was by no means clear what Beijing's "bottom line" would be. A number of published reports revealed what the Chinese *hoped* to convince the Americans they should now agree to. However, it was unclear whether these statements indicated what Chinese leaders regarded as an optimal goal, or what they expected to result from negotiations.

At the end of 1981, just before Holdridge's visit to China, the *People's Daily*, in a commentator's article titled "China Resolutely Opposes Foreign Arms Sales to Taiwan," authoritatively outlined Beijing's basic position:

> On the issue of how to solve the problem of U.S. arms sales to Taiwan, China both sticks to its principles and is also reasonable. Here, a fundamental principle must first be affirmed. This means that in accordance with the principles of international relations and the communiqué on the establishment of Sino-American relations, the United States should properly respect China's sovereignty and should not interfere in its internal affairs and should not sell arms to Taiwan. Under the premise of recognizing this principle, both sides can hold consultations on ways to solve the problem. However, it is regrettable that . . . the U.S. government has in fact tried by every means to deny facts in an attempt to avoid being constrained. With regard to this, we must clearly point out, if you want to preserve and develop Sino-American relations, then the problem of U.S. arms sales to Taiwan must be solved on the basis of properly respecting China's sovereignty.[71]

A few days after Holdridge left Beijing, an article written by the correspondent of Italy's leading Communist newspaper reported that a Chinese source had asserted that China's basic position was as follows:

> If the United States recognizes Chinese sovereignty over Taiwan—the fact that there is only one China and that Taiwan is part of it—if they accept the *principle* [emphasis added] of not selling weapons to Taiwan and of a gradual diminution of sales, then we can permit the sale to Taiwan of certain kinds of weapons—

71. *People's Daily*, December 31, 1981, in FBIS, *Daily Report: PRC*, December 31, 1981, p. B2.

defensive and not "advanced" weapons—for a certain period of time. If they do not agree to this, then we will oppose all arms sales.

The article suggested that there could well be "negotiations" on this question that continued "for months."[72]

Shortly thereafter, a major Chinese Communist paper in Hong Kong published an editorial titled "Grave Moment in Sino-American Relations," which stated that it is a "grim international reality" that U.S.-China relations are now at a serious "danger point." The editorial suggested, once again, that nothing less than U.S.-China agreement on the duration of U.S. arms sales to Taiwan would now be acceptable to Beijing. "Since the unilateral decision of the United States to sell arms to Taiwan," the editorial stated, "U.S. Assistant Secretary of State John Holdridge has made a visit to Beijing. In the bilateral talks, China insisted that this question must be decided by both sides, and that China will not allow anyone to trample on the principle of Chinese sovereignty." After the talks, according to the editorial, "China asked the United States to set a final time limit on the sale of arms to Taiwan."[73]

On March 1, the New China News Agency, commenting on the decade of U.S.-China relations since the Shanghai Communiqué in an article titled "Critical Point in Development of Sino-U.S. Relations," stated:

> China has made great efforts for the solution of the problem of U.S. arms sales to Taiwan. . . . In view of the fact that the Taiwan issue is inherited from history, the Chinese government, while sticking to its principled position, has been very patient and realistic in its negotiations with Washington and has put forward many reasonable and just proposals.
>
> However, the matter has developed to such a point that China is forced into a corner without any options. If the United States insists on a long-term policy of selling arms to Taiwan, Sino-U.S. relations will retrogress.[74]

In the period from January through March 1982, no significant progress was made in resolving or compromising the differences between the Americans and Chinese over arms sales to Taiwan. American officials initially had hoped that it would be possible to reach some sort of compromise with the Chinese by late February, the tenth anniversary of the Shanghai Communiqué. However, after the Americans outlined their position to the Chinese in February, they received no reply for almost a month, and when a

72. "China's Precise Conditions for Dialogue With United States," *L'Unita* (Venice), January 19, 1982, in FBIS, *Daily Report: PRC*, February 10, 1982, p. B1. The reporter hinted that the source was a top Chinese leader, perhaps Li Xiannian.

73. Editorial, "Grave Moment in Sino-U.S. Relations," *Wen Wei Pao* (Hong Kong), February 9, 1981, in FBIS, *Daily Report: PRC*, February 9, 1981, p. W1.

74. NCNA, March 1, 1982, in FBIS, *Daily Report: PRC*, March 2, 1982, p. B1.

reply did come in mid-March, it was reportedly very "tough" and uncompromising.

American press reports indicated that the U.S. government had gone quite far in assuring Beijing that Washington would exercise restraint in arms sales to Taiwan. One article, citing "officials and congressional sources," asserted that "the United States has proposed to China that the two governments issue a declaration in which Washington would pledge not to provide Taiwan with military equipment beyond the quantity and quality of its current arsenal and which would indicate that, if Taiwan and the mainland reconciled differences, there would be no need for additional sales."[75] Whether or not this report reflected the exact nature of U.S. assurances, there was no doubt that U.S. diplomats had outlined to the Chinese a position that went much further in indicating an American willingness to exercise self-restraint than anyone would have thought President Reagan would have approved a year earlier. The Americans were dismayed that the Chinese kept pushing them to take much more far-reaching steps—apparently arguing still that the United States must agree in principle that it should set a cutoff date for all arms sales to Taiwan, which Washington was not prepared to consider. Analysts in Washington began to fear that Chinese leaders, for domestic political reasons, might in fact have little or no room for maneuver or compromise—as the Chinese themselves said was the case. Domestic politics also created certain imperatives and limits on flexibility on the American side. Leaders in Washington decided that they could not postpone indefinitely the sale of spare parts to Taiwan that had been announced in December, just prior to Holdridge's trip to China. On April 13, the Reagan administration formally notified Congress of its intention to sell $60 million of military spare parts (essentially aircraft parts) to Taiwan. Congress could have vetoed this within thirty days, but did not. At first there was real uncertainty about how Beijing would react. The Chinese Foreign Ministry immediately protested on April 14, but Beijing chose not to downgrade U.S.-China diplomatic relations. Chinese officials "took note" of Washington's explanation that the sale involved only spare parts and had been promised to Taiwan before Sino-American talks had begun in November. Their statements implied, however, that if the United States made new sales of actual weapons to Taiwan, China would feel compelled to do more than react verbally. Some Chinese officials main-

75. Bernard Gwertzman, "Haig Meets With Peking Official to Discuss Arms Sales to Taiwan," *New York Times*, April 6, 1982.

tained, moreover, that the United States had pledged to make no new weapons sales to Taiwan while talks on the issue were under way.[76]

As of late April 1982, there appeared to be an impasse in the U.S.-China talks on arms sales to Taiwan. It was apparent that for the impasse to be broken there would have to be greater flexibility on the part of China as well as the United States. And it seemed probable that if the diplomatic-political impasse could not be broken, at some point—perhaps in a matter of months—the United States might sell some new weapons to Taiwan, at which time Beijing could well decide to downgrade U.S.-China diplomatic relations.

In view of the complex history of U.S. links with Taiwan as well as China, the potential volatility of American and Chinese attitudes, and the intractability of many of the basic causes of the differences inherent in the U.S.-China-Taiwan relationship, Beijing's apparent determination to press the United States hard to reach an agreement on limitations of future arms sales to Taiwan indicated that U.S.-China relations had, in fact, reached a "danger point." Moreover, Taiwan's situation and attitudes, and domestic political factors in both the United States and China, imposed serious constraints on all the parties involved in and affected by the Taiwan arms sales issue.

Causes for the Potential Crisis in U.S.-China Relations

One cannot be certain why the Chinese leadership decided in 1981 to press so hard on the Taiwan arms sales issue. Several hypotheses are plausible, however. One is that the Chinese loss of confidence in basic U.S. motives and intentions toward Taiwan, especially from mid-1980 on, led Beijing's leaders to decide that in order to prevent a further drift toward a permanent two-Chinas situation (perhaps with U.S. acquiescence if not active encouragement), China would have to adopt a tougher political position. A second hypothesis, widely accepted among American China specialists (and in effect confirmed by some Chinese officials in private conversations), is that Beijing's leaders believe that the chances of moving toward reunification could well decline as the mainlander leaders who now rule on Taiwan pass from the scene, and that therefore they should do everything possible to initiate a dialogue before Taiwan's top leader, Chiang Ching-

76. Michael Weisskopf, "China Protests U.S. Plan to Sell Parts to Taiwan," *Washington Post*, April 15, 1982.

kuo (Jiang Jingguo), dies. Still a third hypothesis, which is very plausible, is that during 1979–81, despite all the progress made in many aspects of U.S.-China relations, the Taiwan problem became once again a major issue in domestic Chinese policies, and that some leaders in Beijing who may have felt that Deng Xiaoping had been duped by the Americans when he agreed to defer the Taiwan arms sales issue (probably together with others who opposed Deng's domestic policies) demanded a tougher line regarding U.S. policy toward Taiwan.

Changes in China's Overall Foreign Policy Posture

The record suggests, moreover, that, as Beijing became increasingly concerned about U.S. policy toward Taiwan, Chinese leaders began to reassess their overall foreign policy strategy and posture. It appears that some began to have doubts about the wisdom of aligning too closely with the Americans on broad international issues. As U.S.-China tensions concerning Taiwan arms sales rose, there also were increasing signs that Beijing was adjusting its posture on many other international questions.

The Chinese began to be more overtly critical of a broad range of U.S. domestic and foreign policies. From 1978 until 1981, most publicly expressed Chinese opinions about the United States and its policies were remarkably favorable. Beijing's leaders seemed determined to paint as bright a picture as possible of the United States as a society and deliberately played down differences between Chinese and American foreign policy, linking Chinese and American interests to an unprecedented degree.

By the second half of 1981, however, the tone of Chinese discussions of the United States and its policies clearly had begun to change. Once again, Beijing's leaders and the Chinese press were inclined to highlight rather than to gloss over Sino-American differences. The new criticism dealt with both American domestic policies and U.S. foreign policy.

Waning Confidence in the United States

In early January 1982 the *People's Daily*, in an article titled "A Difficult Year," argued that the Reagan administration's policies in general had been unimpressive during the previous year. "In an economic sense," it declared, "things have proved contrary to expectations"; moreover, the article stated, "Reagan's revitalization plan was not well founded and was mostly guesswork."

The article made a sweeping criticism of the narrow view and shortsightedness of the Reagan administration's overall foreign policy. It asserted that his administration's "decisionmaking machinery is not operating smoothly," and U.S. "foreign policy has been marked by a lack of consideration of the overall situation and a lack of consistent guidelines." "In the United States of today," it said, "and the world of today, many things and tough problems can never be solved by just relying on the U.S. president's will or by just relying on the strength of the United States itself. If it is thought that the United States can do whatever it likes and if the United States lacks a farsighted strategic view of the whole world and overlooks the existence and role of various other factors in the world, then it will surely come to grief."[77]

Many Chinese press articles now highlighted U.S. domestic problems—unemployment, inflation and others. For immigrants from China to the United States, one article declared, "actual life in the United States turns out to be quite a blow to them."[78] The analysis presented by China's papers of the economic situation in the entire Western world was extremely gloomy. One article, for example, discussing the "long-term stagnation of the Western economies [which] started in 1974," asserted that "a mood of despondency pervades the whole Western world."[79]

Criticism of Washington's Stress on Arms

One broad criticism of U.S. foreign policy that was particularly striking, in light of the fact that for a decade Beijing had urged Washington to build up its military strength and be tougher in dealing with Moscow, was contained in an article titled "Weakpoints of the United States," which stated: "As a superpower, the United States has another weakness, namely, blindly worshipping weapons and not knowing how to generate mass support."

Although "Reagan claims that the United States respects the sover-

77. Chen Youwei, "A Difficult Year," *People's Daily*, January 21, 1982, in FBIS, *Daily Report: PRC*, January 22, 1982, pp. B1, B2, B3.
78. "Six Major Illusions of the New Chinese Immigrants," *People's Daily*, January 14, 1982 (excerpts from articles in *North American Daily*), in FBIS, *Daily Report: PRC*, January 26, 1982, p. B7.
79. Te An, "Where Is the Way Out?" *People's Daily*, January 14, 1982, in FBIS, *Daily Report: PRC*, January 20, 1982, p. A1.

eignty of other nations, he has consistently displayed an 'unjust' and 'irre-sponsible' attitude towards them," the article asserted. "He has also inter-fered in their internal affairs. Washington's influence is waning in the third world because of U.S. support for Israel, South Africa, and other reaction-ary regimes." An accompanying article on "Moscow's Policy" stated: "In contrast to Reagan's hard-line policy, Moscow has pursued a policy of 'moderate gestures' and 'big sticks.' "[80]

Chinese criticism of the Reagan administration's policies toward third world nations became increasingly sharp over time. "The United States has not established fair and responsible relations with the third world," de-clared one article. "On the contrary, the United States has frequently pit-ted itself against the vast third world countries. . . . Apparently among the advanced Western countries, the United States is the toughest on the ques-tion of North-South relations." It went on to say: "In Central America, the Reagan administration has opposed the Soviet and Cuban intervention in the Central American countries' internal affairs, while posing as the enemy of the local national and democratic movement, trying its utmost to ob-struct changes in these countries which the United States dislikes."[81] Sev-eral articles specifically criticized U.S. policy toward El Salvador.

Doubts about U.S. Relations with Europe and Japan

The Chinese press also began to give increased attention to evidence of growing differences between the United States and its allies in Western Europe and Japan. In general the tone of articles on Europe was sympa-thetic to Western European rather than American views. For example, a deputy director of a research institute attached to the Chinese Foreign Ministry published an analysis in which he asserted: "Western Europe wishes to become independent in every aspect of its foreign policy . . . [and] an increasing number of people in Western Europe believe that in the 80s, the Europe-U.S. alliance must be fundamentally reformed."

The author discussed European desires for détente with Moscow, with surprisingly little criticism:

> The West European countries have tended to emphasize the need to maintain "détente" with the Soviet Union. . . . [They] have considerable economic and military strength, and they have their own calculations for supporting "détente," not entirely resulting from their weakness or the lure and pressure of the Soviet

80. *Beijing Review*, no. 1 (January 4, 1982), pp. 12, 13.

81. "International Current Events," Beijing Domestic Service (radio), February 5, 1982, in FBIS, *Daily Report: PRC*, February 10, 1982, pp. B3, B4.

Union. . . . It is possible, if "détente" is implemented, for Western Europe to impose certain restraint on the Soviet Union and strengthen its position vis-à-vis the United States. Some Europeans believe that in the stalemate between the two superpowers, this policy will provide Western Europe with the key to a greater opportunity for diplomatic maneuvering.[82]

Discussions of U.S.-Japanese relations in early 1982 also highlighted growing problems. A major article in the *People's Daily* was titled "Japanese-U.S. Contradictions Seem To Be Intensifying." Analyzing recent "contradictions" in the fields of trade and defense, the author argued that present conflicts between Washington and Tokyo appear more serious than those in the past. He asserted:

> The future is by no means promising . . . there has been an atmosphere of suspicion between Japan and the United States. People in Japan and the United States are worried that such an atmosphere will consequently lead to a political movement and the friendly relationship between the two countries will be shattered.[83]

"Superpowers" and "Hegemonism"

Articles in the Chinese press increasingly referred once again to the United States as well as the Soviet Union not only as a "superpower" (a derogatory term in China's political lexicon) but also as a country following a "hegemonist policy." One such article asserted: "In Washington there are not only politically blind men, but also a considerable number of Yankee fools who are not blind but are foolish all the same."[84]

Some articles emphasized U.S. weaknesses and inconsistencies in dealing with worldwide problems posed by the Soviet Union. One article stated:

> In its contention with the Soviets over the past year, the United States has not freed itself from its passive, unfavorable position. The reason is its many weaknesses. . . . Negotiations with its allies on many matters have been frustrated as a result of poor handling of ally relations. . . . Due to the many difficulties involved, the Reagan administration . . . could only withdraw from its hardline position. . . . The intensifying rivalry between the U.S. and Soviet superpowers [in 1981] had a continuous impact on the world's hot spots. However, the two superpowers' abilities to influence the development of events declined. . . . The United States and the Soviet Union are clearly not as capable of influencing the

82. Guo Fengmin, "Basic Ideas Behind the Foreign Policies of West European Countries," *Beijing Review*, no. 4 (January 25, 1982), pp. 21–25.

83. Zhang Yunfang, "Japanese-U.S. Contradictions Seem to be Intensifying," *People's Daily*, March 20, 1982, in FBIS, *Daily Report: PRC*, April 2, 1982, p. A1.

84. "Away with Hegemonism," *Hsin Wan Pao* (Chinese Communist paper in Hong Kong), January 15, 1982, in FBIS, *Daily Report: PRC*, January 18, 1982, p. W1.

situation as in the past. . . . Many countries in the hot spots also did not want themselves to be manipulated by the two superpowers.[85]

As 1981 drew to a close, one Chinese journal carried a year-end analysis (based largely on reports from the foreign correspondents of the New China News Agency), which was titled "The Present World Is Very Disquieting." To a striking degree the analysis stressed the failings and weaknesses of both Soviet and U.S. policy. Much of the article was devoted to analysis of the struggles in Kampuchea, Afghanistan, and Poland; the continuing conflicts in the Middle East; and "the pacifist tide" in Western Europe. However, throughout the article, both the United States and USSR were portrayed as being unable to cope effectively with existing problems. "The 'polar bear' [the USSR]has been bogged down in a quagmire in Afghanistan and Kampuchea. Failing to pull itself out from the quagmire, it has no alternatives than to 'drag on' and wear itself out."

The news agency's Washington correspondent contributed this analysis:

U.S. and Soviet military capabilities [are] generally comparable. . . . The Reagan administration takes a stronger stance toward the Soviet Union . . . [but] when a real problem has arisen (for example, the invasion of Afghanistan and Kampuchea), no strong determination is likely to be made, nor any significant measures worked out. . . . The situation is rather passive. . . . [These] tactics are not likely to bring about quick results. The reason is that the United States has shortcomings [and] the minds of its people and the thinking of its allies are unstable and not at ease. . . . [A]weakness often ignored by a superpower is that it has blind faith in arms but does not see the need to rely on the masses and the majority. . . . If the United States does not adjust its policies in good time, its weakness will be more obvious.

The United Nations correspondent added, "While the United States assumes a hard line toward the Soviet Union, the actual policy carried out toward that country has been rather confusing."[86]

Increasingly, the Chinese press tended to blur the distinctions between the two superpowers. Previously, for years Beijing had focused its harshest criticisms almost entirely on the Soviet Union, labeling it as the superpower posing the principal immediate threat to the world, against whom all others should unite. Now some Chinese articles (especially those that dealt with the Taiwan problem) again stressed the similarities of the two superpowers. One, for example, asserted:

85. Xin Wen, "Turbulence and Intricacy," Beijing Domestic Service (radio), January 7, 1982, in FBIS, *Daily Report: PRC*, January 12, 1982, pp. A1, A2.

86. Excerpts from an article in *Liaowang* (a Chinese journal), no. 9 (December 1981), carried by NCNA, December 20, 1981, in FBIS, *Daily Report: PRC*, December 29, 1981, pp. A1–A5.

There are people in the United States who live in the 1980s, but believe that China's sovereignty is limited and that of the United States is boundless. Their conception of American authority reminds people of Brezhnev's theory of limited sovereignty. . . . Is it simply because the United States is a superpower and has a big nuclear arsenal that some Americans claim the right to unlimited power in affairs on Chinese soil?[87]

Discussing the arms race, another article asserted: "The debate over 'who is threatening whom' has no longer been considered as news. Both the superpowers . . . are arguing that . . . each feels militarily threatened by the other. . . . This reminds us of the age-old argument of whether the chicken or the egg came first. It is in the course of this continual wrangling that the arms race of the two superpowers grows fiercer and fiercer, constituting in [an]increasingly serious threat to world peace. . . . It seems that this debate will go on forever and the world will never be able to enjoy true peace."[88]

Changing Tactics in Dealing with Moscow

There was also a noticeable change in tone in many Chinese articles and statements on the Soviet Union. The Chinese press continued strong criticism of Soviet foreign policies and still warned that the Soviet threat remained very serious worldwide. But criticism of Soviet domestic policies clearly declined. The Chinese no longer carried bitter denunciations of Soviet "revisionism" (one explanation being of course that China's own domestic policies had swung in directions that the Maoists had previously denounced as "revisionist"). While still warning against Soviet expansionism, the Chinese now increasingly stressed the domestic and foreign factors constraining Moscow. An article titled "Whither Soviet Global Strategy?" began, for example, with the statement: "The Kremlin staggered into the new year [1982] burdened with problems at home and abroad that defy easy solution." Although the article discussed in some detail the dangers posed by the Soviet Union's continuing military buildup, repeating Beijing's long-standing warnings about the resulting threats especially to Europe and the Middle East but also in "the East," it asserted that

[the Soviet Union's] ailing economy . . . coupled with the protracted war in Afghanistan and the Polish crisis, has more or less shackled the feet of the Soviet giant in pressing ahead with its expansion abroad. . . . Looking at the crystal ball, one may say that there probably won't be another Afghanistan for some

87. "Arrogant Anti-Chinese Elements," *Beijing Review*, no. 50 (December 14, 1981), p. 11.

88. Xiao Ying, "Which Came First—the Chicken or the Egg?," *People's Daily*, January 31, 1982, in FBIS, *Daily Report: PRC*, February 1, 1982, p. A1.

time to come. But unfortunately, temperature in the world's hot spots remains dangerously high and there is always the possibility of new trouble spots coming into being.[89]

A number of developments during 1981–82 raised questions about whether or not Beijing might be modifying its long-standing posture of rigid hostility toward the Soviet Union. There were signs of improvement in bilateral state-to-state relations. At least two leading China specialists in the Soviet government made private visits to China.[90] In late 1981, a Chinese gymnastics team participated in an international meet in Moscow and reportedly had "friendly conversations" with their Soviet counterparts.[91] At the end of the year the director of Beijing radio broadcast greetings to the Soviet people, in which he said, "Dear friends: Allow me . . . to warmly congratulate you on the new year and wish you in the new year lots of happiness, good health and success in your work. . . . We hope that in the new year our relations and friendship will be consolidated even more."[92] In early 1982, a leading member of the Soviet-Chinese Friendship Association made an unofficial visit to Beijing.[93] At about the same time, a Chinese journal stated succinctly: "China is not afraid of the Soviet military threat."[94]

The Chinese also were remarkably silent about the crisis in Poland.[95] Privately, Chinese diplomats admitted that Beijing was far from enthusiastic about the emergence of an independent trade union in any socialist country, but they also stressed that, although the Soviet Union had clearly exerted threatening kinds of pressures on Poland, it had not directly intervened, as it had in Czechoslovakia. They asserted that they opposed outside intervention by either superpower. Publicly, Li Xiannian, a member of the Chinese Communist party's Standing Committee, stated in an interview

89. Tang Tianri, "Whither Soviet Global Strategy?," NCNA, February 6, 1982, in FBIS, *Daily Report: PRC*, February 8, 1982, pp. C1–C2.

90. M. S. Kapitsa and S. L. Tikhvinski.

91. NCNA, November 21, 1981, in FBIS, *Daily Report: PRC*, November 24, 1981, p. C4.

92. Jin Zhao (Director of Beijing Radio), "Greetings to the Soviet People," Beijing Radio (in Russian) December 31, 1981, in FBIS, *Daily Report: PRC*, January 8, 1982, p. C1.

93. *South China Morning Post* (Hong Kong), January 18, 1982, in FBIS, *Daily Report: PRC*, January 18, 1982, p. W1.

94. "Sino-U.S. Relations," *Beijing Review*, no. 1 (January 4, 1982), p. 3.

95. Richard Halloran, "China Refuses to Criticize Soviet Over Poland," *New York Times*, January 31, 1982.

that China opposed "all foreign interference" in Poland and "When we speak of interference, we understand by that all interference."[96]

More important, there were hints that Beijing was at least considering a resumption of the Sino-Soviet border talks that had been suspended following the Soviet invasion of Afghanistan in 1979. On September 25, 1981, Moscow's leaders proposed resuming negotiations.[97] They were fully aware of the new strains in U.S.-China relations and doubtless hoped that these would influence Beijing's attitudes toward talks with the Soviet Union. The immediate Chinese response came in a Foreign Ministry statement which simply stated: "We have always maintained that the boundary question should be settled through negotiations, but owing to reasons from the Soviet side, no agreement has been reached so far. We are studying the Soviet proposal."[98] Near year-end, a Chinese government spokesman then revealed somewhat cryptically that China had "recently responded," adding: "The two parties must prepare themselves well before resuming negotiations. Any date should be discussed through diplomatic channels."[99]

The most noteworthy public statement made by any high Chinese official during this period regarding the possibility of Sino-Soviet talks was one made by party Vice Chairman Li Xiannian, in an interview with the correspondent of the Italian Communist party newspaper *L'Unita* in January 1982. A report from Rome on the interview stated, "In the Chinese view [perhaps it should simply have said 'Li's view'] as it emerged from the interview, the dangerous rivalry between the two superpowers threw ominous shadows over Europe, Japan, and the developing world." Li was quoted as saying: "We well know that the United States remains an imperialist country" even though it is now in a defensive position while the Soviet Union is on the offensive. Paraphrasing Li, the report stated that he reiterated the Chinese position that

> China and the Soviet Union must still find a solution to their border problems. ... China has no impediments to opening a dialogue with Moscow, although such talks would surely touch on the need for a withdrawal of Soviet troops from Afghanistan and of Vietnamese troops from Cambodia. It would not be easy for the Soviets to give an answer to these things.

96. Agence France Press, January 8, 1982, in FBIS, *Daily Report: PRC*, January 8, 1982, p. C1.

97. Dusko Doder, "Soviets Propose to Chinese that Talks Be Renewed," *Washington Post*, October 20, 1981.

98. Agence France Press, October 20, 1981, in FBIS, *Daily Report: PRC*, October 20, 1981, p. C1.

99. Agence France Press, December 28, 1981, in FBIS, *Daily Report: PRC*, December 28, 1981, p. C1.

Li was directly quoted as saying: "We are not against the U.S.-USSR negotiations underway in Geneva, so why should we be against Sino-USSR negotiations."[100]

An Agence France Press report from Beijing on the same interview quoted Li as saying, "We are not setting any preconditions," even though it was inevitable that, in the talks, Afghanistan and Cambodia as well as the "withdrawal of Soviet forces deployed along our borders and in Outer Mongolia" would be raised.[101]

Nothing in these reports suggested that Beijing had significantly eased its stand on the intractable substantive issues that China and the Soviet Union have tried to deal with in intermittent negotiations ever since the border talks started in the 1960s. However, the reports suggested that China might be more flexible tactically in dealing with Moscow than it has been in recent years.

Statements such as Li's seemed to encourage Moscow to step up its efforts to reopen border negotiations. On March 24, Leonid I. Brezhnev himself made a new proposal for negotiations that sounded more conciliatory than any in years. Brezhnev underlined the fact that Moscow rejected the two-Chinas concept and recognized Beijing's claim to Taiwan. He stated that Moscow was prepared to discuss possible "measures to 'strengthen mutual trust' along their border" and "to come to terms, without any preliminary conditions, on measures acceptable to both sides."[102] (In March there were additional direct contacts of significance. Most important of these was a visit by three Chinese economic experts to Moscow to study Soviet management methods.)[103]

The official Chinese response to Brezhnev's March 24 statement was noncommittal. On March 26, a Foreign Ministry spokesman in Beijing said that China's leaders "have noted the remarks" and "firmly reject the attacks on China" contained in them, but he did not say that China had rejected the idea of renewed talks; instead he simply declared that "what we attach importance to are actual deeds."[104]

100. ANSA (Rome), January 8, 1982, in FBIS, *Daily Report: PRC*, January 13, 1982, p. G1.

101. Agence France Press, in FBIS, *Daily Report: PRC*, January 8, 1982, p. C1.

102. Robert Gillette, "Brezhnev Offers Chinese a Way to End Dispute," *Washington Post*, March 25, 1982.

103. Dusko Doder, "Chinese Trip to Moscow May Signal Sino-Soviet Thaw," *Washington Post*, March 18, 1982.

104. See Serge Schmemann, "Brezhnev Presses Overtures to the Chinese Leaders," *New*

Renewed Emphasis on the "Three Worlds"

Of all the changes in emphasis in China's posture on broad international problems that became apparent during 1981, perhaps the clearest were Beijing's strong reassertion of the Chinese concept of "three worlds" (classifying all nations into three groups—the superpowers, the other industrial nations, and the developing countries), its renewed emphasis on China's support for the developing nations (as a self-proclaimed member of the third world), and its increased criticism of U.S. policies toward the third world.

From 1977 through 1979, China had said relatively little about the "three-worlds concept," its press commentaries on North-South issues had decreased, and its rhetoric on such issues was noticeably more restrained than previously. In 1980, however, this changed. The Chinese again gave very extensive coverage to North-South problems, reasserted China's role as a third world leader, and strongly criticized American as well as Soviet policies toward the developing nations.

In the fall of 1981 one major Chinese article strongly reemphasized China's third world ties. "Chairman Mao's strategic conception of the three worlds is correct," it said. "China will always be a member of the third world and never seek hegemonism. . . . Developing relations with the United States does not mean that China supports its erroneous policy toward some third world countries."[105]

Throughout this period, a stream of articles in the Chinese press criticized the Reagan administration's policies on a wide range of third world concerns and North-South issues. In early October 1981, one article, after declaring that the U.S. position on aid to developing nations "caused anxiety and resentment among the developing countries," added: "North-South economic relations is [sic] by no means a simple economic issue. It should be considered from the viewpoint of the immediate international politics."[106] Later in the same month, the author of another article declared that "one of the main weak points of the Reagan administration's foreign policy [in 1981] was that it neglected the important role played by the third world in the present international situation. It overemphasized East-West

York Times, March 25, 1982; and NCNA, March 26, 1982, in FBIS, *Daily Report: PRC*, March 26, 1982, p. C1.

105. Shen Yi, "China Belongs For Ever to the Third World," *Beijing Review*, no. 39 (September 28, 1981), p. 23.

106. "Roundup: South-North Dialogue Seen From World Bank Meeting," NCNA, October 4, 1981, in FBIS, *Daily Report: PRC*, October 5, 1981, pp. A1–A2.

relations or even subordinated North-South relations to those between East and West."[107]

Shortly thereafter, in early November, in an article about the United Nations, the Chinese charged that in the 1950s the United States ("with U.S. dollars in one hand") had "manipulated the veto machine," and declared that this era was forever gone. "At present," the article stated, "the third world countries . . . can neither be bribed nor coerced. They will not take orders from Washington and will not submit to Moscow."[108]

At year-end, an NCNA review of U.S. foreign policy during 1981, titled "Talking About U.S. Foreign Policy," declared:

> Perhaps the most crucial aspect of U.S. foreign policy is that toward the third world countries. There is no denying the fact that the thrust of Soviet expansionism is the most threatening in the third world and the Middle East and South Asia in particular. . . . Still, the question remains whether the United States has the resolve to make bolder adjustments of its policy toward the third world. . . . Often the United States as a great power fails to treat the third world countries as equals and to act impartially toward them all. Those political groupings, whether they are in power or overthrown, are taken as its old friends so long as they are pro-American and anti-Communist. . . . [Washington] often does not scruple to interfere in the affairs of other countries, even at the expense of its own long-term strategic interest. . . . The United States government has proclaimed opposition to hegemonism of any country as its basic policy. Well, it is much easier to oppose the hegemonism of others than to oppose one's own. This perhaps is the crux of the problem of U.S. foreign policy.[109]

Throughout this period, not only did Chinese publications increase their verbal criticism of U.S. policy toward the third world, the Chinese government became much more active diplomatically in support of third world causes, and it became notably more assertive in the United Nations. The most striking example of this was Beijing's decision in late 1981 to fight hard—despite strong U.S. support for a new term for Kurt Waldheim as UN secretary-general—to insist that someone from a third world country be chosen for that post.[110] For the first time, the Chinese used their veto

107. Zhang Dazhen, "Public Opinion in the West on the Reagan Administration's Policy Toward the Third World," *People's Daily*, October 18, 1981, in FBIS, *Daily Report: PRC*, October 21, 1981, pp. B2–B3.

108. Sima Da, "More Money Than Votes," *People's Daily*, November 6, 1981, in FBIS, *Daily Report: PRC*, November 6, 1981, p. B1.

109. Peng Di, "Yearender: Talking About U.S. Foreign Policy," NCNA, December 26, 1981, in FBIS, *Daily Report: PRC*, December 28, 1981, pp. B2, B3, B4.

110. See Edward A. Gargan, "Chinese Widening Role at the U.N.," *New York Times*, October 26, 1981; and Bernard D. Nossiter, "U.N. Vote Propels Ugandan and China to Center Stage," *New York Times*, December 13, 1981.

power in the UN repeatedly until their view prevailed, and, ultimately, they were able to ensure that a third world representative (though not the one Beijing originally had supported) was approved as Waldheim's successor.

Significance of These Trends

The coincidence of increasing strains in bilateral U.S.-China relations over the Taiwan arms sales issue and signs of possible broader changes in China's general international posture was clearly not accidental. As of early 1982 it was impossible to foresee how far the broader changes might go.

Some of the new Chinese criticisms of U.S. policies toward other countries—not only toward the third world but toward the United States' closest allies as well—were unquestionably intended to be oblique criticism of the Reagan administration's policy toward China, especially as it related to Taiwan. Charges that the United States, as a superpower, is prone to interfere in the internal affairs of other countries, frequently violates other nations' sovereignty, supports "old friends" even if they have been "overthrown," ignores the desires of some of its closest supporters to be truly independent, tends to act unilaterally and to impose its own views on others, and (the most bitter charge) on occasion seems to operate on premises close to Brezhnev's doctrine of "limited sovereignty," unquestionably were not simply criticism of U.S. policy toward other countries; they were not very subtle indirect criticism of American attitudes and policies on the Taiwan issue as well.

Yet, despite the mounting criticism of general U.S. policy, the tone of most Chinese statements did not suggest that Beijing had abandoned its desire for friendly U.S.-China ties or had reverted to a policy of hostility toward Washington. On issues other than Taiwan, the tone of the Chinese statements usually seemed to reflect feelings of sorrow or regret more than of anger. Many of the Chinese criticisms, in fact, were no more harsh (and sometimes less so) than those directed at Reagan administration foreign policies by certain critics in the United States or in other Western and third world nations. Moreover, even as the strains in U.S.-China political relations regarding the Taiwan issue escalated to a point of real "danger," U.S.-China economic relations and educational and scientific interchanges continued throughout 1981 and early 1982 to develop in a very positive way. In 1981, U.S.-China trade rose to a new peak (over $5.5 billion), and in early 1982 Beijing opened bidding for oil exploration rights in key South China sea shelf areas to foreign oil companies, including major American companies.[111]

The Chinese continued to assert that they wished to maintain and further develop strong, friendly U.S.-China ties, and in their foreign economic policy in particular they appeared to be operating on the assumption that, despite their new demands for changes in U.S. policy on arms sales to Taiwan, somehow it would be possible to prevent any major setback in overall U.S.-China relations. Privately, however, Chinese diplomats stressed that the outcome of talks on the Taiwan arms sales issue would be crucial, and that, if relations reached an impasse over this issue, the consequence probably would be a downgrading of official relations. Generally, during 1981 and 1982 they argued that a political setback would have an adverse impact on trade and other ties in the future. However, as the impasse over Taiwan arms sales continued without progress toward compromise and as the possibility of a political setback continued, top Chinese leaders began expressing the hope that key economic ties could be protected from the effects of any political setback.

It was very difficult to judge what the long-term significance might be of the shifts in Beijing's broad international posture that accompanied mounting U.S.-China tension over Taiwan. However, it was impossible to exclude the possibility that the shift foreshadowed a gradual move away from—or at least a modification of—the dominant central theme of Beijing's overall international strategy from the late 1960s until 1981, namely the coalescence of a worldwide united front in which the United States and all the other major industrial nations would play key roles in close cooperation with China and as much of the third world as possible.

China's official statements and press commentaries during 1981 and early 1982 certainly did not indicate in any clear fashion that Beijing's leaders had yet decided to alter this decade-old strategy in any radical way; Beijing still labeled Moscow as the main threat to world peace. Nevertheless, many statements did suggest that the Chinese were positioning themselves for possible further shifts in their global posture.

What such a shift might involve, if it were to occur, could be inferred from the kinds of statements quoted earlier. These statements suggested that Beijing's leaders could decide to reemphasize further their theory of

111. See "Foreign Trade with Selected Countries," *China Business Review*, January–February 1982, p. 69; and Christopher S. Wren, "China Opens Oil Search Offshore to Foreigners," *New York Times*, February 17, 1982.

three worlds and their primary identification with the third world, and also stress the two superpowers' similarities rather than their differences, place increased priority on strengthening China's ties with the "second world" (Japan and Western Europe), and take steps deliberately to distance China politically from the United States, underlining Beijing's determination to avoid political dependence on Washington.

In early 1982, while there were many hints that the Chinese could decide to move further in these directions, it remained unclear to what extent these were mainly tactical, designed to remind Washington that Beijing does have options other than increasing its reliance on U.S. strategic and economic support. In part, the hints undoubtedly were intended to exert leverage on Washington to make further compromises on the Taiwan issue, but they clearly were more than that. The change in Beijing's overall foreign policy had not gone so far, however, that the trend could not be checked or reversed by Beijing, especially if compromise on the Taiwan issue could be reached. If the discussions initiated after Holdridge's trip to Beijing could produce a new compromise on this issue, it would not be difficult for the Chinese to renew primary emphasis on the key importance of U.S.-China cooperation and to try to strengthen relations, playing down rather than highlighting the differences between the two countries' policies.

Nevertheless, the clear signs of changes in China's international posture did raise the possibility that Beijing was not only reexamining policy because of the Taiwan problem, but was also—as a result of a reassessment of broad international trends—considering major adjustments in its overall foreign policy. Leaders in China now seemed to view general world trends differently from the way they had during 1978–80. They seemed to have less confidence in the United States' intentions and capabilities, and they appeared to take a less alarmist view of Soviet capabilities.

One important clue to a direction in which overall Chinese policy might move was contained in the statement cited earlier, in which the author (a Chinese scholar close to Beijing's Foreign Ministry) asserted that "some Europeans believe that in the stalemate between the two superpowers," Europe might, through détente, be able "to impose certain restraint on the Soviet Union and strengthen its position vis-à-vis the United States," which could provide "the key to a greater opportunity for diplomatic maneuvering."[112] It is plausible that by 1982 some Chinese felt that in the stalemate between the two superpowers Beijing too might be able, if it adopted more

112. Guo Fengmin, "Basic Ideas Behind the Foreign Policies of West European Countries."

flexible policies, to discover a "key to a greater opportunity for diplomatic maneuvering."

If Beijing does decide that global trends argue in favor of greater flexibility and maneuverability in Chinese policy—whether or not there is a major setback in Sino-American relations—what changes in overall Chinese policy would be likely? Under existing circumstances it is improbable that Beijing would suddenly decide on a dramatic shift of policy comparable to that which took place when the Sino-Soviet split and the initial steps toward U.S.-China détente occurred. What seems more likely is that the Chinese might decide to move cautiously toward a more independent position between Washington and Moscow to try to increase Beijing's flexibility in dealing with both.

Even under such circumstances, there is little possibility that any far-reaching Sino-Soviet rapprochement would occur; however, gradual steps toward a limited détente between Beijing and Moscow would certainly be possible. Nor do the Chinese seem likely, under foreseeable circumstances, to revert to a hostile general policy toward the United States. Even if there were to be a political setback in U.S.-China relations over the Taiwan issue, Beijing probably would still try, to the extent possible, to continue having Chinese trained in the United States and to maintain certain important cooperative economic ties with the Americans, especially in the fields of agriculture and energy and in some high-technology fields as well—though they might turn increasingly to Japan and Europe for the latter.

In March, Deng Xiaoping himself made clear that he hoped U.S.-China economic relations would continue to expand even if there was a setback in political relations. He was reported to have said to Armand Hammer, chairman of a major U.S. oil company, that while there was "no room for a deal" over Taiwan, this issue "will not affect business with China."[113] (Some Americans were less sanguine about the prospect of protecting economic relations from politics, however.)

Assuming no reversion to outright Sino-American hostility and conflict, the Chinese probably also would continue to see some convergence of U.S. and Chinese interests on particular international issues, above all the problem of balancing Soviet power, which they doubtless would continue to see

113. Report by Agence France Press, Hong Kong, March 26, 1982, in FBIS, *Daily Report: PRC*, March 26, 1982, p. B1. See also Frank Ching, "China Won't Downgrade Links with U.S. Over Sales to Taiwan, Peking Official Says," *Wall Street Journal*, April 7, 1982. Ching reports the official interviews stated that, even if there is a downgrading of official relations over future U.S. arms sales to Taiwan, China would hope that it would not affect economic, trade, and cultural relations.

as the greatest potential threat to China's security. Even if their confidence in U.S. policy is weakened, they are likely to continue to view the United States as the strongest global counterweight to Moscow and recognize some continuing parallelism in the efforts of both China and the United States—even if not closely coordinated—to check Soviet expansionism. If so, there would continue to be at least an indirect linkage of Chinese and American security interests.

However, even if all of these judgments prove to be correct, any serious setback in U.S.-China political relations over the Taiwan issue—or any decision by Beijing to deliberately distance itself politically from Washington—would undoubtedly alter the tone of U.S.-China relations and limit the possibilities for expanding U.S.-China cooperation or increasing parallelism in the two countries' policies. A major shift in China's overall international posture, especially if it is perceived to be the result of a political crisis between Washington and Beijing over the Taiwan issue, could have more far-reaching—and more unpredictable—effects on other nations in East Asia. Most of these nations would view the future with greater uncertainty, and virtually all would feel compelled to reassess the regional balance and consider adjustments in their own policies toward the major powers. It is difficult to predict what the long-run consequences would be.

The Immediate Issue: Arms Sales to Taiwan

During 1980 and early 1981, many Americans in and out of the government appeared to believe that the central issue in U.S. policy toward China was whether Washington should sell arms to Beijing. It was assumed by some that the United States, if it chose to do so, could initiate arms sales to China and at the same time continue to sell to Taiwan whatever types and amounts of military equipment Washington decides are appropriate, with little consideration of possible adverse Chinese reactions. Those who held such views also appeared to assume that arms sales and direct military ties were the key to developing a more significant strategic relationship with the Chinese. They seemed to overlook the problems that could arise because of continuing differences over Taiwan, as well as the many uncertainties about how U.S. policy on arms sales to both China and Taiwan might affect the East Asian region as a whole.

By 1982, it was apparent that this approach, which gave higher priority to arms sales policy than to fundamental political issues, was based on serious misjudgments. China's leaders obviously had different views. They were not willing to lay aside political differences, especially over Taiwan, simply because the United States announced its willingness to sell China arms. In fact, they seemed to suspect that by offering to sell them arms Washington was attempting to buy Chinese acquiescence to U.S. policies that Beijing opposed. By 1981, it had become painfully clear that the crucial immediate issue in Sino-American relations was not whether Washington should sell arms to China, but rather whether the two countries could avoid a political crisis and a major setback in their relationship because of differences over U.S. arms sales to Taiwan. At every stage in the evolution of U.S.-China relations since the early 1950s, the central issues have focused on Taiwan; events during 1981–82 demonstrated that this has not changed.

The Chinese decision during the late summer of 1981 to postpone indefinitely the Chinese military mission that Haig had invited to Washington highlighted the fact that, under present circumstances, the strategic significance of relationships between the United States and China depends fundamentally on the nature of the political relationship between the two countries, not on whether direct military relationships can now be expanded.[114] This does not mean that Beijing might not be interested in developing some military ties with Washington and purchasing some U.S. military technology in the future, if existing differences over Taiwan and other issues can be narrowed and if the basic U.S.-China political relationship appears to be on a sound, sustainable, basis. It does mean, however, that in the period immediately ahead the priority goal of U.S. policy toward China must be a restoration of greater mutual confidence in the political relationship between the two countries. One prerequisite for this clearly will be further compromise on the Taiwan problem.

What are the prospects for compromise? At present, they are uncertain. If both countries are genuinely determined to repair what is now a seriously strained relationship, if both are prepared to take into account the complex domestic as well as international factors that impose constraints on the other, and if both show realism and flexibility in the talks now under way, it should be possible to reach new understandings that both countries can live with. But these are important "ifs," and finding a basis for compromise will not be easy.

114. See Don Oberdorfer, "Absence of Peking Arms Buyers May Be Hint to U.S. on Taiwan," *Washington Post*, September 18, 1981; and Richard Halloran, "Reagan and Peking Aide Skirt Arms Issues in Talks," *New York Times*, October 30, 1981.

Leaders in both Beijing and Washington are in many respects hostages to history and domestic politics. Moreover, the intrinsic complexities and dilemmas that the Taiwan problem poses are so great that no solution, in any final sense, is conceivable in the near future. At best, American and Chinese leaders can only hope to contain the problem and support trends that move in a direction acceptable to both. If both sides fully recognize this, reaching some sort of new understanding should be possible. However, it is possible that talks on the Taiwan arms issue will be difficult and prolonged. If they are, they will create continuing strains that, at a minimum, will complicate the task of restoring mutual confidence between Washington and Beijing. If a complete deadlock persists, there will be a continuing danger that at some point Beijing will decide to downgrade official Sino-American ties (probably if and when Washington makes a new sale of weapons to Taiwan). Such an outcome would increase the possibility that Chinese leaders would reassess their general foreign policy and move further in directions suggested by recent statements emanating from Beijing.

Since 1972 successive American administrations, recognizing the importance of good relations with China and accepting the necessity for compromise on the Taiwan problem, have moved cautiously toward acceptance of the principle of one China, while making it clear that Washington will continue to oppose any attempt by Beijing to reincorporate Taiwan into the Chinese polity by force. However, the U.S. government has hedged—by using deliberately ambiguous phraseology in both the Shanghai Communiqué and the communiqué on normalization of relations—on whether or not it really recognizes Taiwan, even in principle, to be a part of China, at least in the sense that Beijing means, namely a part of the territory of the People's Republic of China. (Beijing has consistently maintained that Washington already in fact has done so, but some of its recent statements show that it really doubts that this is the case.) Moreover, in its public statements Washington generally has been vague on whether it believes that an eventual reassociation of some kind by Taiwan with the mainland would be a desirable development. From the perspectives of Washington and Taipei, it has seemed preferable to leave open what the long-run future of Taiwan might be. But this inevitably has kept alive Beijing's suspicion that the U.S. policy in reality might be a disguised two-Chinas policy.

Moreover, as Beijing charges, certain U.S. policies doubtless have not only tended to perpetuate the status quo but have also, intentionally or not, reinforced the inclination of Taiwan's present leaders to reject all of Beijing's proposals for direct contacts or any steps to initiate a dialogue. In spite of Beijing's new flexibility in its proposals for reunification and the lack of any foreseeable likelihood of a direct military threat from China to Taiwan, the United States has continued arms sales to Taiwan on a sizable scale in a desire to be responsive to Taipei's fears of a military threat at some time in the future. These arms sales during 1979–81 reinforced Beijing's suspicion that, while ostensibly recognizing one China, Washington in fact might favor a permanent separation of Taiwan from China. (The scale of U.S. arms sales to Taiwan has subsequently been reduced—but not before the issue had become highly contentious in U.S.-China relations.)

Future U.S. Policy

What further adjustments should the U.S. government now be willing to consider in its policy toward both China and Taiwan and specifically in its policy on future American arms sales to Taiwan? What assumptions and goals should they be based on?

Despite Beijing's increased dissatisfaction with U.S. policy and its current intense pressures on Washington, the United States should stand firm in its position that it will oppose any use of force in "solving" the Taiwan problem. Beijing doubtless will continue to view this as interference in China's domestic affairs, but nevertheless should be able to live with it—in part because China is unable, in fact, to consider a military solution at present and in part because it now emphasizes that its goal is peaceful reunification.

Washington can and should base its policy on the premise that for the foreseeable future the Chinese are unlikely to use military means to try to achieve reunification, for many reasons. Not only does China now lack the military capability for an amphibious invasion of Taiwan, it would take many years for it to acquire such a capability, and there is no sign that it has even started the kind of military buildup that an invasion would require. Equally important, if the Chinese were to revert to a policy based on the use of force or even military threats against Taiwan, they would put at risk their basic relationships with Japan and many other countries (including the United States). These relationships probably will continue to be of great importance to China's modernization, as well as to its national security interests, for many years. Beijing's leaders recognize this, and they are not likely to risk undermining relationships with all of these countries— whatever the precise military balance in the Taiwan Strait area—unless

China's domestic as well as foreign policies undergo a drastic turnabout. Some observers speculate that China, with its large submarine fleet, theoretically could try to compel Taiwan to capitulate by imposing a blockade on the island; this too seems highly unlikely, in view of the political costs as well as military risks that such action would involve.

The Chinese could of course eventually revert to a more belligerent rhetorical posture and a more threatening military stance if they conclude that their campaign for peaceful reunification is totally unsuccessful. This would not pose any immediate real threat of an invasion. It would, however, raise tensions in the Taiwan area and have destabilizing effects throughout the region.

U.S. policy also should be based on the premise that Beijing's present leaders are apparently realists, and while they hope to start a dialogue with Taiwan soon, they do not in fact expect that reunification will be achievable quickly. One cannot be certain that this is the case, but it is probable—and policy can only be based on probabilities. If this is the case, what explains the seeming sense of urgency characterizing China's recent moves toward Taiwan, and why are the Chinese now pressuring Washington with such vehemence that U.S.-China relations today are severely strained? The most plausible answer is that China's leaders became increasingly worried during 1980–81 about the direction of trends that could affect Taiwan's future. Increasing apprehension about a drift toward permanent separation appeared to revive the Taiwan problem as an acute issue in domestic Chinese politics. The primary immediate objective of Beijing's pressure on Washington seems to be to halt any such trends and, if possible, to start trends that will increase the possibility of eventual reunification.

Not only should the U.S. government be more sensitive than it has been in the recent past about Beijing's concern, but American leaders also must now ask themselves what long-term trends are most likely to contribute to peace and stability in the Taiwan area and therefore be in the U.S. national interest. A strong case can be made that over time the prospects for stability in the Taiwan area should improve if and when some kind of process of interaction between China and Taiwan begins, perhaps starting with economic and other nonofficial contacts but leading eventually to some kind of political dialogue; unless such a process eventually takes place, there is a high probability that in the long run there will be renewed dangers of conflict in the area.

The United States cannot itself ensure that such a process will begin, and it certainly is not able and should not try to determine whether such a process will lead over the long run to reunification, to looser links between Taiwan and China, or to some other sort of gradual accommodation between the two. Therefore, the official U.S. position should remain what it has been since 1972, that the Taiwan issue eventually must be settled peacefully by the Chinese themselves.

The reality of the situation is that the possibility of peaceful accommodation between Beijing and Taipei will not improve significantly until Taiwan's leaders and a significant portion of the island's population recognize that their interests will be better served in the long run by some kind of relationship with Beijing than by unrelenting hostility and tension. Whether Taiwan eventually is persuaded of this will depend in part on future developments within both China and Taiwan and in part on the way in which any future interaction between the two actually evolves. However, if Beijing is persistent in its efforts to demonstrate that it is genuinely prepared to take the interests and desires of people on Taiwan fully into account in any proposals for relinking the island with China and to offer Taiwan a high degree of real autonomy, and if important economic ties of mutual benefit gradually develop between China and Taiwan, an increasing number of people on the island may be willing to consider the advantages of some kind of reassociation with China. They may conclude that there is little basis for believing that an independent Taiwan could be viable in an environment in which it would not only face increasing Chinese hostility but probably would also find itself more isolated internationally than at present. However, at present people on Taiwan do not believe that China would tolerate genuine Taiwanese autonomy (and many would object even to the concept of "autonomy" under Beijing's authority). Beijing therefore faces a difficult task in persuading them that ties with China would be more desirable—or at least less undesirable—than Taiwan's other options in the long run.

Although U.S. policy cannot determine future China-Taiwan relations, it certainly is not irrelevant to the issue, and U.S. positions and actions clearly will influence whether or not some process of interaction between Beijing and Taipei eventually begins—as leaders in both China and Taiwan well know. The U.S. government should now make it clear that its policy is based on the premise that steps toward direct contacts and ultimately some kind of dialogue and mutual accommodation between China and Taiwan are highly desirable. In shaping its own policies, the United States also should try to help in whatever ways it can to create a political climate that encourages rather than discourages the start of a process lead-ing in this direction.

Washington should not, however, try to *force* Taiwan to start a dialogue with China. Any attempt to do this would almost certainly be counter-productive. Not only might Taiwan harden its opposition to any contacts with China, the effects could be destabilizing on Taiwan itself, and serious new strains in existing nonofficial U.S. ties with Taiwan would result. Nor should the United States consider trying to mediate between the two. If it did, it probably would eventually become a scapegoat for both. Neverthe-less, the U.S. government should now make it clear to both Beijing and Taipei that it believes an eventual mutual accommodation is not only desir-able but necessary for the preservation of peace and stability in the area.

If Washington does this, the initial reaction of leaders in Taiwan doubt-less will be negative, and there is certainly no guarantee that Taipei would soon consider changing its present policies. Moreover, Beijing might feel that Washington still had not gone far enough, and continue to charge that the U.S. government is interfering in China's domestic affairs. Neverthe-less, clarifying the U.S. position in this fashion is desirable because, by adopting such a posture, the U.S. government would indicate clearly for the first time what it believes is necessary for long-run stability in the area.

Washington also must continue its efforts to convince Beijing that the United States does not and will not pose any challenge to China's sover-eignty. Opinions differ among knowledgeable American China experts as to what this will require. Some argue that the official U.S. position taken at the time of normalization, that Washington "acknowledges the Chinese position" that Taiwan is a part of China, is still the soundest one for the United States to maintain. They believe that no reformulation of the U.S. position is necessary. They point out that Beijing has not insisted that other major powers be totally explicit on the Taiwan sovereignty issue. It is much more important, they argue, to convince Beijing that the concrete policies pursued by Washington do not encourage trends toward two Chinas than it is to modify the formal position that Washington defined and Beijing found acceptable at the time of normalization. They maintain that defining the U.S. position more explicitly now could create new legal problems for the U.S. government, complicate the task of maintaining existing nonofficial relations with Taiwan, and give Beijing new legal arguments and leverage for pressing Washington to end all arms sales to Taiwan.

In the opinion of other knowledgeable China experts, however, a more explicit U.S. position on the sovereignty issue may now be desirable and even necessary to overcome the doubts of Chinese leaders about U.S. long-term intentions, as well as to break the existing impasse over the Taiwan issue. Persons holding this view argue that if the United States were itself to acknowledge in principle that Taiwan is a part of China, it would simply be accepting the official position that has consistently been maintained ever since the Potsdam agreement of 1945 by Chinese leaders, including those in the Nationalist regime.[115] Taking this step would not be without some cost, they acknowledge; but they argue that even if it were to strengthen somewhat the legal basis on which China's leaders argue that it is illegitimate for Washington to sell any weapons to Taiwan, in reality it would not alter the present situation significantly. They note that Beijing already maintains that Washington should accept the principle that it should sell no arms to Taiwan. They argue that the issue of U.S. arms sales to Taiwan is more political than legal, and any compromise on the issue will be based more on political calculations than on legal judgments (or legalistic arguments) made by leaders in Washington and Beijing.

In light of all these considerations, it appears that redefinition of the U.S. position on the sovereignty issue probably is less important at present than other adjustments in U.S. policy, especially ones affecting the issue of actual arms sales to Taiwan. However, if it appeared that adjustment of the official U.S. position on the sovereignty issue would make a major contribution toward achieving a new basis for compromise between Washington and Beijing, it should be seriously considered *if* (and it is an important if) there were reason to believe that such a compromise would enhance the prospect for a gradual, peaceful, evolutionary change in U.S.-China-Taiwan relations and decrease the likelihood of future political crises over the Taiwan issue.

Clearly the most important issue now requiring a redefinition or clarification of American policy is the issue of future U.S. arms sales to Taiwan. What should Washington's position now be regarding such sales? The arguments against simply agreeing to set a cutoff date are strong. If the U.S. government were to do this, both the leaders and population on Taiwan—and many others, not only in East Asia but elsewhere—would probably see it as a sign that the United States had agreed in effect to pull the rug from under Taiwan at a specified date and was prepared to force a rapid accommodation between Taipei and Beijing. No process of mutual accommodation between the two is ever likely to succeed unless it is the result of a

115. See Barnett, *Communist China and Asia*, pp. 388–89, 410.

gradual process, and announcing a cutoff date is not the way to encourage such a process.

The effects on Taiwan could be highly destabilizing. Both local business-men and foreign investors would probably start immediately to hedge against an uncertain future and begin withdrawing assets from the island, which could have very serious adverse effects on the economy. Political cleavages and tensions between local Taiwanese and the mainlanders might well intensify, since some Taiwanese already suspect that Taipei's main-lander leaders might someday suddenly strike a deal with Beijing, even though this seems very unlikely. Many might conclude that they should try to take political action to prevent any sellout. It is also conceivable that instead of feeling that they were compelled to accommodate to Beijing, Taiwan's leaders might decide to declare independence—and even attempt to develop an independent nuclear weapons capability. It is virtually cer-tain that there would be an extremely hostile reaction in Taiwan to the United States, probably leading to a serious deterioration of existing nonof-ficial relationships.

It is possible that Beijing's leaders do not believe that these things would occur, but are convinced instead that Taiwan's leaders, facing a cutoff of U.S. arms, would have no alternative but to begin negotiating terms for reunification. It is also conceivable that Chinese leaders do believe that announcement of a cutoff date would have a tremendous shock effect on Taiwan, but do not believe that Taiwan could consider taking steps such as declaring independence or going nuclear. Whatever views Chinese leaders hold, the actual effects of announcing a cutoff date would probably work against everyone's interests—including those of China's leadership.

While Washington should not agree to a cutoff date, it should be pre-pared to modify present policy regarding arms sales to Taiwan if it wishes to avoid a major setback in U.S.-China relations. The question is: how and to what extent?

It is now essential for the U.S. government to somehow convince Beijing that although it will continue arms sales to Taiwan because of "historical" reasons (which the Chinese say they have been willing to take into ac-count), it will exercise greater restraint in doing so. At the time of normal-ization "the United States made clear its intention to continue the sale of defensive weapons to Taiwan on a restrained basis."[116] Now it should indi-cate convincingly that, in light of the reduction of tension in the area and in

116. "Diplomatic Relations With the People's Republic of China," news release, Depart-ment of State, December 1978, p. 2.

the expectation that tension will further decline, the United States does not plan to sell more sophisticated military equipment to Taiwan and in fact anticipates that it will gradually reduce the level of arms sales.

The linkage between the anticipated reduction of U.S. arms sales to Taiwan and the expectation that tension in the area will diminish (especially if and when contacts between China and Taiwan increase) should be implicit rather than explicit, however, since Beijing has objected to any explicit linkage by Washington. According to plausible press reports, when American officials in early 1982 communicated to the Chinese a new U.S. position generally along these lines, the Chinese rejected it, arguing that linkage of U.S. arms sales to future developments in China-Taiwan relations would represent a new form of U.S. interference in Chinese domestic affairs.[117] In defining official public U.S. policy, Washington obviously should take account of Beijing's view on this question if it wishes to maximize the possibility of achieving a new compromise that can prevent a setback in U.S.-China political relations. However, it is important that actual reductions in future U.S. arms sales to Taiwan be related to improvements in the prospects for peace and stability in the area.

Even if the United States adjusts its position in all the ways suggested, it is by no means certain that the Chinese will be persuaded to accept it as a new basis for repairing and improving U.S.-China relations. The modifications in U.S. policy would fall far short of China's recent public demands. If the Chinese insist on what press reports suggest are their maximum demands, a serious setback in U.S.-China relations is likely.

An Evolving U.S. Position

In fact, in early May 1982 it became clear that during the previous two months the Reagan administration had shown increasing flexibility and had begun adjusting its policy along the lines suggested above, but it re-

117. *Wall Street Journal* correspondent Frank Ching reported that a knowledgeable Chinese official told him that the Americans had [in Ching's words] "proposed linking the reduction of arms sales to Taiwan to tranquility in the Taiwan Straits and to the peaceful unification of Taiwan with the China mainland" but that "China has rejected this proposal." Ching quoted the official as saying that this would constitute "double interference" in Chinese affairs (that is, attempting to tell China how to resolve the unification issue as well as continuing arms sales to Taiwan); see "China Won't Downgrade Links With U.S. Over Sales to Taiwan."

mained unclear whether the Chinese also would show the flexibility required for any new compromise.

The evolution of the U.S. government positions during early 1982 was clarified by the texts of three letters from Reagan to Chinese leaders released during a visit to China May 5–9 by Vice-President George Bush.[118] His visit, proposed by Reagan in a letter to the Chinese a month earlier, came at the end of a trip to Japan, South Korea, Singapore, Australia, and New Zealand.

Reagan's three letters included two dated April 5: one to Vice Premier Deng Xiaoping stated that the Americans "fully recognize the significance" of Beijing's proposals for peaceful reunification of China and Taiwan, and the other, to Premier Zhao Ziyang, stated that "we welcome your peace proposal." Reagan's letter to Zhao also stated that he had told Huang Hua in November, "We would expect that in the context of progress toward a peaceful solution, there would naturally be a decrease in the need for arms by Taiwan." (Press reports said little about the contents of the third letter, which Bush hand-carried to party chairman Hu Yaobang, except that it emphasized Reagan's commitment to a one-China policy.) However, despite these conciliatory statements made by the United States during April, Chinese public statements made at the same time had shown little sign of increased flexibility on Beijing's part. When Bush arrived on May 5, Deng Xiaoping declared: "We hope that through your visit . . . we can completely sweep away the shadows and dark clouds existing between us."

American officials stressed that no one expected Bush to be able suddenly to resolve U.S.-China differences over arms sales to Taiwan, but it was clear that the central purpose of his trip was to try to break the impasse and point the way to a new compromise. At the time Bush left China, there was little basis for judging whether his talks with Chinese leaders—described as "frank," "candid," and "sincere"—had improved the prospects for resolving the U.S.-China impasse. Bush stated that he had "a much better understanding of the depth of feeling" that the Chinese "have on these issues," and "a much clearer perception" of the Chinese position on Taiwan, and that he was returning to Washington with "some specific ideas" to discuss with the president. And Ambassador Arthur W. Hummel,

118. The following data, including the quotations, are from Christopher S. Wren, "Bush Fails to Sway China on Taiwan," *New York Times*, May 9, 1982; and Christopher S. Wren, "Bush Leaves China With New Ideas for Resolving Taiwan Arms Dispute," *New York Times*, May 10, 1982.

Jr., told journalists that a "very high-level exchange of views of this sort produces better understanding and lays better groundwork for an eventual solution." But there was still no clue as to whether the Chinese had modified their demands, or whether the prospects for compromise had significantly improved.

It is possible that the Chinese will prove to be flexible and realistic enough to conclude that Washington cannot accept their maximum demands, that changes in U.S. policy such as those suggested above would be significant, and that compromise on their part is unavoidable if they genuinely wish to continue developing mutually beneficial relations with the United States. One basis for hoping that they will reach such conclusions is the fact that the costs for them of a serious deterioration in U.S.-China relations could be very high. Another is the fact that in some comparable situations in the past they have shown a capacity to be both realistic and flexible. Yet on other occasions, when Chinese leaders have strongly felt that their principles or sovereignty were violated, or that other powers were bullying them, they have been rigid and uncompromising even when they have had to pay a high cost. To be confident in predicting how China's leaders will act in the present situation, one would have to know much more than it is possible to know about their real attitudes toward the United States at present; what their basic fallback position would be on the Taiwan arms sales issue, as well as the degree to which this issue has become embroiled in domestic Chinese politics; and how much Beijing's assessments of broad international trends have changed.

If the impasse over arms sales to Taiwan results in a downgrading of U.S.-China diplomatic ties, the priority task of U.S. policy for some time thereafter will of necessity be one of damage limitation. The immediate aim should be to minimize the impact of this symbolic political setback both on bilateral U.S.-China economic and cultural relations and on the East Asian region as a whole. A longer-term aim clearly should be to continue the search for a basis for new compromises that will make possible the repair of basic U.S.-China political relations.

If a new compromise on the arms sales issue acceptable to both sides can be reached, what should one expect relationships between the two countries to be immediately thereafter? It is conceivable, but by no means certain, that the existing tensions would then rapidly subside, and that a relatively smooth process of strengthening bilateral political and economic ties would resume. It is also possible that under the best of circumstances the strains in the relationship that have developed since 1980 will take time to repair, and that new initiatives by both sides will be required to gradually rebuild a sense of mutual confidence in the relationship.

If a compromise can be reached, the United States should thereafter attempt to initiate a variety of new moves that would help to rebuild such confidence. An exchange of visits between President Reagan and Premier Zhao could be one important confidence-building step. Not only would such an exchange have major symbolic significance; it could help to increase the understanding of both these key leaders (neither of whom was involved in the complicated task of building U.S.-China ties in the 1970s) of the complexities, problems, and opportunities inherent in the relationship between the two countries. In terms of broad policy, Washington should place special emphasis on the need to take new steps to try to strengthen U.S.-China economic relationships in ways that will help Beijing move forward successfully in its modernization program.

However, even if a new compromise is reached that helps to get U.S.-China relations back on track, and new attempts to repair and strengthen ties thereafter are successful, it would be naive to assume that the Taiwan problem will therefore have been laid aside for an indefinite period. In a sense, the United States may simply have bought more time, and that probably is all one can hope for in dealing with a problem as complex and intractable as the Taiwan issue. If a process of direct interaction between China and Taiwan can be encouraged, and if further development of economic and other bilateral ties between the United States and China gradually creates a stronger web of interlocking interests, one can hope that it will be possible to prevent future political crises over the Taiwan issue. However, since even under the most optimistic assumptions any significant process of mutual accommodation between Beijing and Taipei is likely to take many years, the Taiwan issue clearly will long remain a potential time bomb that could be triggered by decisions made in Beijing, Taipei, or Washington. Trying to defuse the issue or at least manage it successfully should be a continuing priority objective of U.S. policy. Washington also should try in every way it can to induce both Beijing and Taipei to try to defuse the issue through a process of genuine compromise and accommodation and to avoid actions that could precipitate new crises over the issue.

U.S.-China Military Ties

The strains that developed in U.S.-China relations during 1981–82 over arms sales to Taiwan put on ice, at least for the immediate future, questions relating to U.S. strategic and military relationships with Beijing, including arms sales to China. It is clear that if there is a major setback in U.S.-China relations, or even just a prolonged period of continuing strain, there will be no significant new steps in the military field in the near future. However, if the present impasse can be broken and political relations repaired, questions about further development of military-strategic ties will doubtless be placed on the agenda of leaders in both nations once again. What approach should the United States then take to these issues?

It is clear that the maintenance of good relations with China is of strategic importance to the United States. U.S.-China détente altered the security environment in East Asia in many ways that lessened the dangers Washington faces in the region, and a serious deterioration of relations could exacerbate problems throughout the area. However, events since 1981 suggest that U.S.-China political relations have not yet been sufficiently consolidated, and that there is not yet sufficient convergence or parallelism in the policies of the two countries, to justify consideration of extensive military relations. Even under optimal conditions, there are not likely to be many opportunities soon for really close coordination of American and Chinese policies on many critical issues. It was not realistic to expect this even during the 1978–79 period. In light of the apparent recent trends in Beijing's broad foreign policy as well as in U.S.-China relations, the possibilities for coordination already have diminished. Washington can and should try to work toward a greater degree of parallelism, especially in policies toward Korea and Southeast Asia. At a minimum, it should try to prevent any further widening of existing differences. This will be more important strategically than any military relationships that might be developed during the next few years, even though one cannot expect rapid success. Nevertheless, if U.S.-China political ties can be gradually repaired, the arguments for developing certain kinds of military links will probably become stronger once again.

It definitely is in the U.S. interest for China to be secure. Today it is fairly secure in some respects; in others, it is not. China possesses the largest army and third largest navy and air force in the world. However, much of the equipment that these forces possess is inferior to that of Beijing's potential adversaries; a great deal of it is obsolete. Although Beijing's forces and its defensive strategy for using them make it unlikely that any other power could conquer the country, China remains vulnerable to various military threats, for example, moves to detach portions of Chinese territory or strikes aimed at key military installations or industrial centers.

The Chinese do not appear to believe that actions of these sorts are likely in the period immediately ahead, but they cannot and do not ignore the possibility of such threats.

The primary aim of Beijing's current efforts to modernize its military establishment is to improve its defensive capabilities step by step in order to deter and if necessary counter such threats. However, China's present leaders wisely see this as requiring a very long process. Today they give highest priority to the need to strengthen the Chinese civilian economy. Because of this, they actually have reduced China's military budget substantially in recent years.

Nevertheless, they obviously hope to improve their ground, air, and naval equipment over the next ten to twenty years with the aim of acquiring an ability to defend China at its borders, instead of relying on a "people's war" strategy that calls for pulling back and ceding parts of Chinese territory temporarily to any attacker. Under the slogan of "people's war under modern conditions," they have begun to move slowly in this direction and to modify their defense doctrine in marginal ways.[119]

There is little possibility, however, that the Chinese will purchase sizable amounts of military equipment abroad from any source in the foreseeable future, in part because of economic constraints and in part because of China's determination to avoid dependency on any other nation. But they are attempting to obtain new technology and knowledge that will help them both to upgrade their own production of military equipment and to use the equipment they have more effectively. Over the next few years they may attempt to obtain, through licensing, the rights to produce some foreign-designed military equipment, and conceivably they may purchase certain items of foreign-produced military equipment that they need most urgently, such as modern antitank and antiaircraft weapons.

A case can be made that if the United States is sympathetic, as it should be, to the desire of China's leaders to improve their defense capabilities gradually, it should be prepared to authorize the sale of selected defensive weapons as well as certain types of advanced technology of possible military use—as in fact the U.S. government already has offered to do. Yet it is by no means clear that it would be in the best interests of either the United States or China to sell China arms on any sizable scale if the Chinese—contrary to present expectations—showed an interest in buying them.

If U.S.-China relations are improved to such an extent that Washington

119. See Jonathan D. Pollack, *China's Military Modernization, Policy, and Strategy*, P-6041 (Santa Monica, Calif.: Rand Corporation, 1980), pp. 8–12.

and Beijing decide to resume discussions of this possibility, the American government should, before proceeding far down this road, undertake a comprehensive study of what the *long-term* impact is likely to be on U.S. and Chinese relationships with many other countries and areas, including the Soviet Union, Japan, Korea, Southeast Asia, and South Asia. Extensive U.S. arms sales to China, or other military relations, undoubtedly would have a major political impact regionally, which could well stimulate reactions by others that Washington would not like to see, without necessarily having any great near-term effect on the real military balance in East Asia. Some conceivable reactions could increase tensions in the region or create new instabilities. Efforts to establish very close U.S.-China military links might evoke responses from some countries that could seriously affect the regional balance in the long run. Moreover, the effects of overdramatized U.S.-China military ties might even pose new dangers to China's security in the short to medium run, instead of enhancing either American or Chinese security interests. It is not possible here to analyze all of these possibilities. However, a simple recognition that growing U.S.-China military ties could involve such risks and have real political costs as well as possible benefits argues for caution in trying to expand such ties.

Assuming that overall U.S.-China political ties improve once again, the U.S. government may feel it desirable or even necessary to show a continued willingness to make some sales of selected arms and technology to the Chinese. But if it does sell arms, not only should the items sold be carefully selected, the scale should also be limited. There should be no unrealistic expectations, moreover, that these sales will lay a basis for close coordination of the broad foreign policies of the two countries. It would in general be preferable for the Chinese to purchase arms from other sources if they decide to buy from abroad. Several European nations have indicated a willingness to sell certain weapons to China; if these countries were to make such sales, the international repercussions would be much less than if the United States were to do so.

In considering any major steps toward expanded U.S.-China military links, U.S. policymakers should take into account not only the possible long-term impact on the East Asian region as a whole, but also possible complications in bilateral U.S.-China relations. There obviously could be some significant benefits resulting from steps to involve the leaders of Beijing's military establishment (which is extremely important politically in China) in U.S.-China relationships more than they have been to date. If the defense establishments in both countries strongly support the goal of strengthening political relations, the prospects for gradually achieving this goal could improve. Even if close coordination of American and Chinese policies is not likely in the foreseeable future, developing better mutual understanding and limited cooperative military programs might help to narrow some of the existing differences in the two countries' policies. Moreover, even limited U.S. assistance could help to enhance China's security, thereby perhaps contributing to regional stability.

However, attempting to expand military ties extensively under present circumstances, when the future of U.S.-China political relations remains uncertain, would in a sense be putting the cart before the horse. Creating sound, sustainable political ties should precede developing major military links, not vice versa. Moreover, there would be a danger that some Americans and Chinese would soon develop unrealistic expectations and assume that if military ties are expanded broad policy differences should be significantly lessened and unresolved political issues—above all, the Taiwan issue—should be laid aside. Since this is not likely to happen, the result could be severe disillusionment, which could intensify the adverse reactions if either Washington or Beijing were then to take actions of which the other disapproved.

This danger is greatest on the American side. It is not only possible but likely that many U.S. leaders, especially in Congress, would expect that increased military cooperation with China, especially major weapons sales, would mean that the Chinese should be much more "reasonable" and willing to compromise on the Taiwan issue. But in light of Chinese statements made during the past year, this seems unlikely. One can envisage, in fact, a "Catch-22" situation evolving. If U.S.-China military cooperation and arms sales grow, so too in all probability will pressures (both from Taipei and from the U.S. Congress) to increase the level and sophistication of weapon sales to Taiwan. But if Washington were to sell larger quantities or more advanced versions of military equipment to Taipei, this probably would trigger another political crisis in U.S.-China relations, which could abort any attempts to expand cooperative military ties between Washington and Beijing. It is difficult to see how it will be possible to resolve the dilemmas inherent in U.S.-China-Taiwan relationships in the period immediately ahead.

For all of these reasons, the United States should exercise great restraint in its military relationships with—and arms sales to—China as well as Taiwan. In developing U.S.-China relations, the priority goals of both Washington and Beijing now should be to manage the Taiwan problem successfully, strengthen bilateral political and economic ties, and narrow the existing differences between the foreign policies of the two countries. If either Washington or Beijing overstresses the importance of broadening military links at the present stage in the development of relations, this is more likely to complicate the bilateral ties as well as the multilateral relationships of the two countries than to cement the foundations for a sustainable, long-term relationship.

U.S. economic policy toward China will be of critical importance in any effort to strengthen political relations—assuming the Taiwan arms sales issue can be defused. The highest priority in U.S. policy toward China in the period immediately ahead should be to do all that Washington can to assist the Chinese in their efforts to solve their basic economic problems and to maintain domestic political stability—which will depend fundamentally on the country's economic performance. A second priority should be to try through diplomatic means to broaden the areas in which American and Chinese policies are complementary or parallel, especially in dealing with potential East Asian conflict areas such as Korea and Southeast Asia, but also in policy toward many other countries and areas. Whether or not progress can be made in expanding U.S.-China economic relations and in developing parallel diplomatic approaches to dealing with East Asian conflict areas will be much more important to the interests of both nations—including their strategic interests—than efforts to broaden military ties in the years immediately ahead.